GENESIS MOMENT

ANSWERING YOUR HEART'S CALL FOR FREEDOM

BY

JUSTIN STRECKER

This book is dedicated to my loving wife Jordan who has been my biggest source of encouragement and my support through all the trials of life and ministry. I love you and I am so thankful for you.

CONTENTS

Forward

There is a call today for authentic and honest leadership. This book will offer current leaders and future leaders hope and freedom. Today leaders are under attack just as they have been for centuries. Now more than ever people need to know that true freedom is offered through Jesus' sacrifice on the cross and through the application of God's Word. Society does not need any more news about leaders who have given way to immorality and have fallen to the wayside because of hidden sin. Nor should there be leaders who abuse their power and hurt those they are leading because of their inability to live in humility. Society needs to know that leaders can be trusted, not because of their own will power, but because of God's creative power that can be experienced by anyone who hungers and thirsts for righteousness.

It's not just the leaders that need to experience freedom in their hearts. I believe the desire for true freedom exists in the hearts of almost everyone today. Yet I believe that many people struggle to live an abundant life because of pain and cyclical or besetting sin patterns. It is my prayer that this book will provide the insight and tools you need to give you the freedom to live authentically and transparently. Only then will you truly experience love as you were intended to. I believe that all things are timed perfectly in God's kingdom and the fact that you are reading this book is another example of that perfect timing.

As a child I used to wonder about the possibility of the most common things potentially containing the cures for the worst diseases known to mankind. I remember looking at the center of a

Bic pen that I had pulled apart, and thinking, "I wonder if pen ink might cure cancer?" It may seem like a foolish question. Yet, because some things are so common, I thought it was very possible that we could easily be overlooking something revolutionary.

As I sat one night with a friend and discussed the contents of this book I realized that my childlike wonder had now become a reality. Every heart calls out for freedom, and discovering that freedom cures any addiction, heals any pain, and gives life a fresh start. The discoveries that are revealed in the chapters that follow show how the enemy has tried to take away our hearts' ability to dream and live as God intended, and there is nothing closer to any of us than our own hearts. What was profound about my questioning of pen ink is the fact that your heart and its re-creation is the cure to the deadliest of diseases – spiritual heart attacks.

In the pages that follow, it will be my purpose to expose the spiritual heart attacks you have suffered just like the millions of other people whose hearts remain captive and burdened. By exposing the root causes and allowing God's Word to reveal the truth, it will also be my aim to lead you into your own Genesis Moment; it's the moment when the miracle of freedom dawns in your heart.

Freedom for your heart to live and to love is the key to living the abundant life that Jesus came to give. John 10:10 says, *"The thief comes only to steal and kill and destroy. I came that they may have life and have it abundantly."*

Chapter 1

A Fresh Start

Everyone is born into addiction.

It's a very bold statement, wouldn't you agree? Addiction is a word that we are all familiar with and brings with it thoughts of alcohol, tobacco, pornography, drugs, and sex. However, we know today there are so many more addictions than just those five mentioned. You might be reading this book because you know there is some unfinished business in your life that needs to be addressed. You might be a pastor involved in a main stream ministry who cannot overcome the draw to your computer or the devastation you experience every time you give in to the temptation of pornography. You may be able to avoid the computer for periods of time, but your mind is an arena of vivid fantasy that fuels your desire for satisfaction.

This book isn't just for men addicted to pornography. This book is for every person who was born into a world where our desires began to mislead us from the beginning. You might be a woman who cares for her family and stays involved in the local church, but inside you are filled with depression and hopelessness. You may be seeking satisfaction and contentment through your addictions to shopping, or eating, or gossiping.

You may be a man or woman who is so driven for success that you haven't stopped at anything to achieve your goals. You may be someone who is immersed in hobbies and recreation as you continue to search for satisfaction. The list is almost endless of the ways we as humans strive to meet our own psychological and emotional needs. Unfortunately, the process we choose before ever meeting Jesus, results in patterns that become so regimented we are unable to see the deadly grip they hold on our hearts.

I know you are reading this book because there is something going on inside your heart that tells you there should be more to this life and to your relationship with Jesus. As far as your concerned, the pastor's words on Sunday don't make sense week after week as you hear about being a new creation in Christ, only to struggle and fall into the same pattern of sin time and time again. You know there is an abundant life, but you haven't found it to be true for you. My hope in writing this book is to help you discover the Truth of God's Word about your struggle and to provide you an opportunity to take responsibility through action in obedience, believing He alone can set you free. I want to lead you to your Genesis Moment.

You need the hope of freedom and you need to know that God is faithful to His Word. God's grace for our salvation is a gift given, unearned, and unwarranted. However, the freedom God offers to His children in this life is conditional, just as it always was for the children of Israel. Genesis 17:1-2 *"When Abram was ninety-nine years old the Lord appeared to Abram and said to him, 'I am the Lord God Almighty; walk before me, and be blameless, that I may make my covenant between me and you, and may multiply you greatly.'"* The blessing of the Lord remains conditional upon the obedience of His children. Jesus repeated this in the gospel of John as He explained the importance of obedience and its connection with loving the Father and enjoying freedom. John 8:31-32, *"'So Jesus said to the Jews who had believed him, 'If you abide in my word, you are truly my disciples, and you will know the truth, and the truth will set you free.'"*

It is a lie to believe that you will enjoy freedom from sin in this life without fulfilling your responsibility to obey. We know that the power and ability to obey are provided only by the Holy Spirit (Romans 8:11), but this does not remove our responsibility to use our God-given will to deny the flesh and obey His commands. There is some practical work scattered throughout the chapters of this book where you will be tasked with writing out and sharing intimate details of your life. This practical work will be the fulfillment of God's command for confession in James 5:16. Inherent with obedience is blessing. I hope you find it encouraging that this book is not just an idea to think about, but offers you the "how to" of walking in obedience and experiencing your very own Genesis Moment.

Addiction

What about the first statement that I made "Every person is born into addiction?"
Have you ever considered the possibility that God placed within us an insatiable flesh knowing that we could never be satiated apart from Him? What if human life was created to crave, created for a holy addiction? In the right relationship with God, this would be a craving for the One who made us, breathed life into us, lives with us, and desires intimacy with us on the deepest levels. What if a holy addiction brought about life changing power, healing, and miraculous signs that caused people to find peace and contentment in all circumstances? What if that addiction brought a sense of significance and security you never thought possible and fueled your desire for life's purpose as never experienced

before? What if the "high" all people search for in sex, drugs, pornography, alcohol, and tobacco or any other possible "pain killer" can only to be found in the right addiction?

Addiction may have many medical definitions, but we could simply say that an addict believes that he has found the most powerful stimulus, producing the greatest "high" (the greatest amount of epinephrine released into his system) that will ease the emotional, physical, or spiritual discomfort he was experiencing just before the "high". The reason it is an addiction is because it does not produce the greatest "high", it does not satisfy the emotional, physical, and spiritual longing. Instead, it leaves the person in a state of wanting more, so he or she must return to it again and again to keep the "high" going. All addictions by their nature leave people in a state of loss, and so the addicted person thinks he must look for a way to get a better "high", and this is why addictive behaviors are always increasing, more self-destructive, and eventually destroy a person, and ultimately a society.

So what would the right addiction look like? Would it not be finally experiencing the true contentment and satisfaction that all addicts are looking for? Would it not completely satisfy the emotional, physical, and spiritual longings? Are not addicts looking for THE thing that will finally ease all their pain? What if the right addiction was the ONLY thing that had the power to bring total contentment?

The addiction I speak of is a holy addiction to God, through the sanctifying work of the Holy Spirit, for the obedience to Jesus Christ (1 Peter 1:2). He alone offers the stimulus that will allow us to experience the proper contentment that will never leave us wanting – and that stimulus is His presence which can only be found in a true love relationship with Him through faith in

Jesus Christ. All people are born into addiction because we are all born with a sin nature seeking satisfaction in the things of this world – but not all people will live as addicts because a true love relationship with Jesus Christ offers freedom. The addictive behaviors you have today, when captured by Jesus' love, will be your strengths tomorrow as you live for Him.

Acquiring this holy addiction will be dependent upon your desire to have Jesus re-create your life. Your Genesis Moment will come at the appointed time when Jesus speaks His re-creative word of miraculous change over your life. It will be the moment healing breaks forth and you are immersed in God's love as you never thought possible. Healing is promised in God's Word to all those who will obey Him. If you are up for the challenge, you will experience contentment and intimacy in ways you never thought possible.

A Bigger View of God

Today we as individuals suffer from the same problems that we witness throughout the history of the people of Israel. The fathers would begin to seek their own way and would begin raising their children apart from the commands of God. Today America is suffering greatly from the effects of generational sin. The church is suffering from the effects of generational sin and in too many congregations the words of 1 Peter 1:18 ring true, *"...knowing that you were ransomed from the futile ways inherited from your forefathers."* It is time for drastic change in the men and women of America's church. It is time for us to recognize God as He reveals Himself – not as we think He is. We need to look honestly at who we truly are. We need a realistic and humble view of how God views our sin. And finally, we must believe in God's desire to truly dwell intimately with us!

Who is God to you? What is God to you? My guess is that you probably fit into one of the following four categories:

1. Righteous – saved by grace
2. Religious – living in tradition
3. Receptive – seeking spiritual answers
4. Rejecting – denying salvation by Jesus alone

If you are righteous – you have truly received the gift of salvation and believe that Jesus Christ is the Messiah and you are truly born again and destined to spend your eternity with God. But though you have been saved, you find yourself stuck in a sin pattern that seems hopeless. You don't know why you continue in those cycles of sin and why you continue to have these desires that don't line up with God's Word. You have tried all the 1-2-3 steps you can think of to rid yourself of this behavior, but still it raises its ugly head. Maybe you have overcome this sin pattern or addiction for a period of time, only to be let down when it returns. There is hope for you in God's promises!

If you are only religious, you may have been raised in a church most of your life hearing all the Bible stories you could handle in Sunday school. You know all the right answers when anyone asks you a spiritual question. You can quote the Scriptures, you can pray the prayers, and you appear on the outside to be better than most. The problem is you still have a desire for sin. You have never come to a place in your life that you are willing to give up every single sinful act to God. You have been "playing church." There is also hope for you in God's promises!

Or maybe you are receptive but unsure. You may have been recently introduced to the idea of salvation. You got invited to church by some "Christians" and you heard them talk about getting "saved." The message you heard was that if you're not saved then you won't be in heaven, you'll be in hell. Then they told you that if you just pray this prayer you will be "saved" – and so that's what you did – the act of praying a prayer, just like the act of making your breakfast! And now you're wondering, "Why isn't anything different? All these Christians could ever talk about was getting me 'saved.' I did it, but now what? They don't seem to care about me anymore, now I'm just one them…kind of, except they don't look any different than my other friends, they don't talk any different, and they are still going to the bars, sleeping with each other, and getting drunk every weekend. They're worse than most of my other friends. What in the world is this getting 'saved' thing anyway? I can't stand fake people – see this is why I never wanted to come to church in the first place." If you're the one who could make this statement right now, you are right. As I said, the church has fallen into the trap of being handed an empty way of life from our forefathers. Church is the not the answer. Christians are not the answer. Jesus is the only Answer. There is hope for you in God's promises!

Or you are just rejecting Jesus altogether. Like every other person on this earth, at some point in your life you have been hurt – hurt deeply by those that are or were closest to you. You have lost any real trust you ever had, and the world has taught you to simply protect yourself and get the most out of this life that you can. You may have met Christ, and maybe you haven't, but from your point of view nothing is safe and especially not a relationship with someone you can't even see. I completely understand and I pray you keep reading because, there is hope for you in God's promises!

Created for Intimacy

Something happens when we finally get the picture of who God is. We become very insignificant – reduced to but a vapor before the Almighty Creator! Isaiah refers to us as flowers that wither, and as grass that is swept away by the very slightest breath of God. How true it is – have you ever stood in temperatures nearing 25 or 30 degrees below zero? If you have, you quickly realize that if you didn't have a place to warm yourself you would eventually die in those temperatures. The same is true if you have ever sat in a sauna. At nearly 150 degrees the body can only withstand the temperature for an hour before shock will set in and eventually cardiac arrest. Ultimately we as humans must exist within a 70 degree window – we are just like flowers in a greenhouse, the only difference is that God created a cosmic sized greenhouse called Earth in which we find our existence. Psalm 39 says that man at his greatest state is but a vapor before an almighty God.

And yet despite our individual insignificance, our individual importance is of cosmic proportions to the very One that made us. We were created in the image of God – you've probably heard that a thousand times. But let's look at it with fresh eyes. Genesis 1:26 says *"Then God said, 'Let Us make man in Our image, in Our likeness, and let them rule over the fish of the sea and the birds of the air, over the livestock, over all the earth, and over all the creatures that move along the ground.'"* Did you catch it? He says *"Let US make man in OUR image, in OUR likeness..."* Who is God talking about? He is talking about the plurality of His being – we were created by the Lord who is One as Deuteronomy 6:4 tells us. The Hebrew word for used for "One" is in the plural tense. We were created out of a perfect relationship between God, the Holy Spirit, and Jesus Christ – the Father, The Spirit, and the Son.

Let me share with you an imperfect picture of God's plurality that exists within the three persons of God who is yet One. To define the term "person" a Trinitarian understanding was used in the 4th and 5th centuries. Person is not defined as a human, but rather a center of consciousness. God created male and female in His image. He contains three separate centers of consciousness in the Father, Son, and Spirit. Yet, these three centers of consciousness are always aligned, always aware, and always in sync within the Godhead, thus they continually and eternally operate as one.

Whether male or female, all human beings are made up of three main parts. First, in order to be an everlasting being we must have a heart and a soul, which is our spirit. Secondly, to cognitively understand the world around us, we must have a mind. And thirdly, the heart, the soul, and the mind must be housed somewhere and thus we are given our body, which is our flesh and blood. Our existence is an image of God's plurality. However, without our perfected relationship to God, our centers of consciousness – heart, mind, and body – do not align or remain in sync with God. I'm sure there are many times when you knew something was right in your heart, but you reasoned it away in your mind, and carried out a different action in your body. In God, the Father, Son, and Holy Spirit always operate in unison and never apart from one another.

God the Father is the Heart and Soul, His form is a Spirit, and His name is Yahweh, He is "I AM" (Ex 3:14). The Holy

Spirit is the mind of God (John 14:17), He alone searches the deep things of God (1 Cor 2:11). And Jesus Christ is the flesh of God (Heb 1:3)! All three are spoken of individually in Scripture, and are also complete in and through one another. Jesus says in John 14:6, *"I am the Way, the Truth, and the Life. No one comes unto the Father except through me."* Jesus is saying that any person who goes to the Father must have the *Way* in his heart, must have the *Truth* in his mind, and must have the *Life* that houses the presence of God, or there is no possibility of entering into a relationship with Him.

God is the Way. Inside of each of our hearts God placed a longing that beckons us to come back to Him. Romans 1:20 says, *"For since the creation of the world God's invisible qualities – His eternal power and divine nature – have been clearly seen, being understood from what has been made, so that men are without excuse."*; Psalm 33:15, *"He who forms the hearts of all, who considers everything they do."* This place in a human's heart is formless and void before God occupies it. This void is where the enemy of God's creation – Satan and the kingdom of darkness – has brought the attack. By appealing to our deceitful desires he has convinced people to fill the void with earthly things to lead us away from our heavenly inheritance. The only thing capable of filling each void is God Himself, and unless He fills us, we will always fail to be content.

The Holy Spirit is the Spirit of Truth, He convinces, convicts, and confirms the things that we do with our lives (John 16:7-9). We only understand the mind of God by being students of His Word. We must, through the constant use of God's Word, become mature, as we are told in Hebrews 5:14. 1 Corinthians 2:1 says, *"Now we have received not the spirit of the world, but the Spirit who is from God, that we might understand the things freely given us by God."* Our mind is the center of conscious thought, and it is our thoughts that are so easily attacked by our enemy, the kingdom of darkness. Only when God places in our minds His Truth, by His Spirit, are we able to understand His ways and walk in obedience.

Lastly, Jesus is the Life. God in plurality became flesh and blood to walk this earth as an example of who we need to be – and we must imitate Him (Ephesians 5:1, 1 John 2:6). He chose to be perfect in all the areas of His life, born without sin; He is God! Jesus chose to put the Way in His heart. He said in Luke 2:49 as a twelve year-old boy, *"'Why were you searching for me?' He asked. 'Didn't you know I had to be in my Father's house?'"* In John 5:19 He says, *"I tell you the truth, The Son can do nothing by himself; he can do only what he sees his Father doing, because whatever the Father does, the Son also does."* Throughout the Gospels, we are reminded over and over of Jesus' understanding of the Scriptures. He studied the Scriptures and often repeated and quoted them as He spoke to the Pharisees and to the people He encountered. He was perfecting His mind by the Spirit. Matthew 3:16b says, *"At that moment Heaven was opened, and he saw the Spirit of God descending like a dove and lighting on Him."* By placing the Way in His heart, and filling His mind with the truth of God's words through the Spirit, Jesus chose to be perfect in His flesh. Hebrews 4:15 says, *"For we do not have a high priest who is unable to sympathize with our weaknesses, but we have one who has been tempted in every way, just as we are – yet was without sin."* Jesus was perfect in His life as an example for us. He was perfect in the Way, as He loved the Father perfectly. He was perfect in the Truth, as he learned and meditated on God's Word through the Holy Spirit. He was perfect in His Life as the Spirit gave Him power, because he had been tempted and tried, yet chose not to sin. Hebrews 5:7-9 says, *"During the days of Jesus' life on earth, He offered up prayers and petitions with loud cries and tears to the One who could save Him from death and He was heard because of His reverent submission. Although He was a Son, He learned obedience from what He suffered and, once made perfect, He became the source of eternal salvation for all who obey Him."* This is why Jesus tells us in Matthew 5:48, *"Be perfect, therefore, as your heavenly Father is perfect."*

The plurality of God exists in perfect intimacy – the picture of family, and it is in His image that we have been created.

Father	Holy Spirit	Jesus Christ	= Trinity
Spirit	Spirit	Spirit	= ONE in Spirit
Way	Truth	Life	= Jesus Christ
Heart/Soul	Mind	Flesh	=Man& Woman

So why were we created? We were created for God's pleasure – to be intimately connected in a love relationship with Him that would bring Him honor and glory, Revelation 4:11, *"You are worthy, our Lord and God, to receive glory and honor and power, for You created all things and by Your will they were created and have their being."* Colossians 1:16, *"For by Him all things were created; things in heaven and on earth, visible and invisible, whether thrones or powers or rulers or authorities; all things were created by Him and for Him."* Just as God lives in perfect intimacy, He created us so that we could also enjoy His perfect intimacy through the gift of His Son.

17

Our Hero

Jesus Christ is a gift we will never be able to understand. This is how crazy God's love for you really is! John 3:16 *"For God so loved the world* (YOU!) *that He gave his one and only Son that whoever believes in Him shall not perish but have eternal life."* Not only that, but He took it a step further! Romans 5:8 says *"But God demonstrated His own love for us in this: While we were yet sinners, Christ died for us."* God not only sent Jesus to be born, but Jesus willingly died for you, because He doesn't want to be separated from you for eternity! Jesus knew you were created for a relationship with Him and He wants you.

Jesus offered Himself in obedience to His Father's will because He knew we could never save ourselves. He didn't want us to be beaten, to be shamed, to be treated like scum, spit on, scorned, and eventually killed, so He did what any Hero would do. He put Himself in the way – Jesus took the beating, and He paid with His life because He loved His Father and His Father's children that much! Romans 6:23 finishes by saying *"...but the gift of God is eternal life in Christ Jesus our Lord."* Our salvation is an overflowing gift from God out of this love offering that Jesus gave back to God the Father in His death. Do not be deceived that Jesus held you or I as His motivation for death – He couldn't have, or He would have sinned. He held the Love of His Father above all when He obediently died a sinner's death.

God loved us enough to give us Jesus Christ, and Jesus Christ loved God enough to die, and out of their perfect unity – we are offered salvation through Jesus' obedience! I have to say Hallelujah to that! Oh but how victorious is our Hero! Oh death where is your sting, for death could not handle our Hero! And on the third day, He rose victoriously from the grave. You want to talk about a lover, someone to be enamored with? That is why Jesus Christ must become and remain our first love. Only He could do what He did for us. We will be forever in awe of the Cross, and we will never be able to understand fully what salvation cost God. It was there that sin died, and forgiveness became available to the whole human race.

You may be asking yourself; "How can someone as bad as I am ever be forgiven?" It is because God's love is greater than sin. He took your sins into account before you were ever born, and He still died to pay the penalty for them, so that you wouldn't have to, even though He knew all the wrong you would do! Knowing this, you must repent, turn away from your sin by faith, knowing that Jesus is your only hope for salvation. He will never force you to take it, and yet it is His gift that allows you to take it. You must love Him enough to make this decision, seal it in your heart and make it your own. Ephesians 2:8-9 says, *"For it is by grace you have been saved, through faith – and this not from yourselves, it is the gift of God – not by works, so that no one can boast."*

If you have just made the decision to repent by faith and receive the gift of salvation for the first time with sincerity you need to tell someone. Romans 10:10 says it is with the mouth we confess and are saved because that is the action of belief. Start by telling the person who you know has been praying for you. Even the angels are praising God for the salvation of your soul. Welcome to the family of Christ! If you don't have a church that you attend, pray that God will lead you to the fellowship that He wants you to be a part of. As Hebrews 10:25 says, do not forsake assembling with the church.

In this new relationship Jesus will start filling your life with His work, and you my friend, are in for the ride of your life!!

The moment you accept this truth in your heart, that deepest place inside you, where you know that you know – you are forever connected intimately with God and destined to spend your eternity with Him. It is only from the foundation of this relationship that you can then move toward the freedom you long for. Salvation is our first Genesis Moment. But for many, the struggles of sin patterns remain and so beyond salvation you must press on toward God's creative power and pattern as He longs to set you free and make you whole – your next Genesis Moment.

Saved and Struggling

Just as we began this chapter, you may be the person who is truly saved, but continues to battle the sins that so easily and cyclically entangle you. As I said, salvation by grace is a gift, but freedom from your bondage is a series of conditional choices to obey. Unfortunately, when we come to know Christ in this relationship, our old ways do not suddenly disappear. Quite the contrary, the sinful ways that are deeply rooted in us are now just more visible and glaring in appearance because Jesus is the light of the world and shines His light on the darkness in our lives. It is the sinful nature that often wins the battles in our life early on because it is the part of our lives that we have fed the most by pleasing the flesh. The bad habits we have developed, the addictions we have used to cope with our emotional pain, the sinful movies, sinful music, time spent in the world, the bar, the clubs, sleeping around, wasting time on useless activities, etc. have all fed our sinful nature. It is now a beast in your life that wants to be fed. The only way to change its power over you is to starve it.

Your spiritual life, the part of you that was brought to life by faith in Jesus has been fed very little since you were only accustomed to feeding the beast of sin. It would look like a little field mouse in comparison to the lion you have fed for so many years. As you can imagine, if you start starving a lion, he is going to fight you for his food, and depending on how strong he has become, he will win at times. You must feed your spirit the Bread of heaven (God's Word) to counterattack the beast of sin in your life. As you feed your spirit with the things of God, it will grow rapidly and soon will be stronger than the beast of sin. As you starve the beast of sin, he starts to get fatigued and loses the battles because he is weak. Eventually the beast of sin will starve to death and the Lion of Judah will reign continuously in your life.

When you believed and were saved you were given the Holy Spirit who occupies you. He is the power it takes to starve sin and feed the spirit. This pictures the instruction from God's Word in 2 Corinthians 4:10-11, *"always carrying in the body the death of Jesus, so that the life of Jesus may also be manifested in our bodies. For we who live are always being given over to death for Jesus' sake, so that the life of Jesus also may be manifested in our mortal flesh."*

If you truly desire freedom, you will begin today to find ways to starve your flesh. As we walk through the remaining chapters we will take a look at the reasons why you are entangled as you are. We will look at the examples from the Bible of people who fell by believing the same lies that you believe. We will lay out practical steps and writing assignments to engage your heart, soul, mind and strength in discovering the places that have been damaged in your life. A view worth seeing is preceded by a journey worth making. This will be difficult, but the reward of freedom and contentment apart from the plaguing sin in your life will be worth every step. The goal of Jesus' ministry was first to make dead people live, but His ministry didn't stop there; it went on to make live people whole, in order to present them as pure and mature before the Father. Until a person is made whole, holiness is out of reach. Wholeness and holiness can only come through Jesus Christ. If you have the desire for freedom, Jesus promises to grant you freedom and give you a fresh start in life through your own Genesis Moment.

Keep a journal of all your writing assignments, thoughts, and prayers as you walk through this book. When you get to the other side of these struggles it will serve as an altar of remembrance of God's power to change your life.

Reflections:

1. After reading this first chapter, can you clearly identify the areas of your life where you are struggling to live a life of freedom? If so, can you identify by name those addictions, tendencies, activities, or personality traits? Write them out as the Lord brings them to mind and keep them in your journal.

2. What new revelations about Jesus have come to you as you read about the Trinity and the design of your life to be intimate with your Hero? Summarize in a few bullet points the Scriptures that revealed Jesus to you in a new way and meditate upon Him.

3. On a scale of 1 – 10 how would you rate your level of contentment today?

Chapter 2

What Went Wrong?

The second step toward freedom is to gain an understanding of where your problem began and how it formed such strong roots in your life. A problem is never solved until its source is identified and corrected. Today we have a lot of information and a lot of tactics to help men and women stop certain behaviors, but in so many cases those tactics fall far short of curing the source of the problem. We must thank God that He revealed to us through His Word the source of man's problems. All through the Scripture God tells us the importance of man's heart. In Jeremiah we are told of its deceitfulness and desperation to please the sin nature. But because of Jesus' death and resurrection God has chosen to place within man a new heart through salvation and continues the work of transformation through sanctification.

The Heart

I heard someone say recently that we are not human beings with a spirit, but rather we are spirit beings with a body. Just think for a moment about the metaphysical parts of your life. Metaphysical just means that these are the parts that are not visible to the human eye, but are very much real in existence and experience. The metaphysical parts of your life are your heart, your soul, and your mind – I do not believe that anyone would deny that their life contains each of these components. Although they are invisible to the eye in form, they can be evidenced through the physical reaction of the body to various stimuli.

Understanding that these are parts of our makeup we should then organize them in relation to our behavior. Your heart is the source of all of your motivation for action. Your mind is one of the sources that your heart will draw from before forming motivation for action. Your will is your choice in your mind to carry out your motivation into action, or inaction, though you still may have the motivation. Your soul is your created personality, emotions, and mannerisms which affect how your actions are interpreted by the outside world. The path for every decision we make can be mapped from its originating point in the heart – decided on in the mind – and carried out through the soul – by the body – producing a response – affecting the soul – judged by the mind – and finally owned by the heart. This repetitive process produces our opinions and beliefs which are stored in our hearts, affecting future motivations and decisions, and ultimately defining our behavior. We see this in Jesus' words in Matthew 12:34, *"For out of the overflow of the heart the mouth speaks."*

Since the heart is the source, it is my intention to help guide you to rediscovering your own heart through the Word of God and the power of the Holy Spirit. My prayer for you is that you can say honestly, "At any cost to my way of life, I desire total freedom, and I am willing to do whatever it takes with You Jesus." If you can honestly say that, I am very excited for you because God, in Hebrews 11:6, says, *"And without faith it is impossible to please God, because anyone who comes to him must believe that he exists and that he rewards those who earnestly seek him."*

Addiction and its antithesis, contentment, are both contained within the heart of man. Lies believed, opinions owned,

24

and actions repeated leave people still wanting more, and with every unfulfilling result, the efforts are only increased to find what is missing – all the while fortifying and solidifying the blindness caused by these lies. This is the way that 2 Corinthians 4:4 tells us, *"The god of this age has blinded the minds of unbelievers, so that they cannot see the light of the gospel of the glory of Christ, who is the image of God."*

The Problem

So what went wrong? The answer - we all suffered heart attacks as young children. Today one of the leading causes of death is the physical heart attack, which happens when a person's heart seizes and stops pumping blood through the body resulting in death. We have an enemy who understands how important the spiritual heart of man is because it is the source of salvation and love for the Savior. Satan wants nothing more than to take away the ability for each human heart to love. He has devised a plan of epic proportions in generational sin. Parents who have parted from God's commands are likely to hurt their children, often inadvertently, in an effort to shape their external behavior. Deuteronomy 6:4-9 says, *"Here, O Israel: The Lord our God, the Lord is One. Love the Lord your God with all your heart and with all your soul and with all your strength. These commandments that I give you today are to be upon your hearts. Impress them on your children. Talk about them when you sit at home and when you walk along the road, when you lie down, and when you get up. Tie them as symbols on your hands and bind them on your foreheads. Write them on the doorframes of your houses and on your gates."* In the process of generational growth, the attacks on young children's hearts come like a barrage of enemy arrows.[i]

Just as physical heart attacks are a leading cause of physical death; spiritual heart attacks are the leading cause of spiritual death in all of us.

The addiction you may be dealing with today is not a result of your inability to curb your behavior, but is the result of heart attacks you suffered as a child. Today your first step up this mountain of healing is to admit you have a problem bigger than you can handle. Too many of the tactics and methods offered today to curb behavior only deal with the ability to follow a program. Jesus did not come to give us better programs to overcome under our own ability, but to help us see our inability, and to provide His Spirit to miraculously overcome.

Jesus shows us throughout His ministry that until a person has a sincere desire to know the truth, He will not commit to revealing the truth. The woman at the well in John 4 speaks the truth to Jesus about her situation, and seeing her desire for truth, He shares Himself as the living water for her and for those in her community. The Pharisees in Luke 20 ask Jesus under what authority He does the things they have witnessed. They are not asking because they desire to know the truth, but rather for the purpose of trying to trap Jesus in a condemnable sin. He responds with a question for them to test their hearts. He asks whether John's baptism was from heaven or from men. Afraid of the outcome from either possible answer they default to "we don't know." Jesus shows us a very important truth in verse 8; *"And Jesus said to them, 'Neither will I tell you by what authority I do these things.'"* Before you can move toward the healing and freedom your desire, you must determine whether or not you really want to know the truth.

Too many times I have spoken with people who are afraid to admit they have a problem bigger than they can handle. They think they can set themselves free. Pride causes them to think more highly of their spiritual condition than Jesus does, and instead of dealing with truth, they continue to fight and battle with their behavior, never coming into the contentment and peace that Jesus offers to those who will humble themselves.

What is it that you run to when you need to make yourself feel better? Is it pain killers, a glass of wine, a beer, sexual encounters, or pornography? Or is it shopping, eating, gossiping, dating, golfing, getting the attention of men, getting the attention of women, or pursuing same sex attraction? Or is it being the boss, being the center of attention, pursuing the next tailgate party, or being extremely spiritual so that everyone notices? Or would you rather isolate yourself to avoid possible pain? Or do you jump from one relationship to another without finding any satisfaction? It can be any number of self-fulfilling activities.

The reason people do not find freedom and contentment is because they are often unwilling to admit that the fun they pursue is actually sin because it is used in the place of relying on Jesus alone. You will first have to acknowledge that these cyclical patterns in your behavior are areas that you cannot change, but that you believe Jesus can. You must start with your heart and seek to know the truth as God offers it before you find yourself in the position of the Israelites in Isaiah 1:11-15. Read it for yourself and see how God judged their hearts, not their outward religion.

The Source

As we unpack the effects of the spiritual heart attacks we suffer, the following diagram will help you map the damage from the attack to its source. Once we have the source identified we can begin to use God's Word to counter the attack.

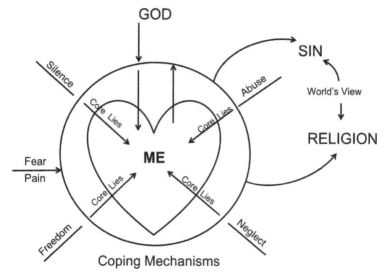

Coping Mechanisms

The diagram represents the heart that God places in each one of us when we are formed in our mother's womb. That placement is represented by the arrow from God into the heart of "ME". Since we learned that God created us for intimacy with Him, the arrow back to God represents the relationship He desires with each person He has created. Unfortunately, before our hearts are able to return to God in a love relationship, we are often subjected to pain. The pain that has the greatest effect on our lives is the pain that is tied to our deepest wants and desires, which are often found in a child's dreams. Our enemy knows the vulnerability of children as they develop and he sets out to bring the greatest pain during these formidable years.

Every human heart is formed by God and within every human heart rests a unique understanding of beauty and mystery, just as God placed it there. Think about the individual nature of beauty and mystery in your life. Imagine you are given the task of sitting beside a lake in the Colorado Rockies and recording the beauty of the sunset as you watch it light up the sky. Now imagine placing any other human being that has ever lived beside you watching the very same sunset with the very same task. The two pieces of paper recording the beauty of that sunset would never be word for word identical. We are created unique for a reason – that we will come to understand the greatness of God through the beauty and mystery He placed within us and that is only fully realized through our relationship with Him.

As we unpack the heart of man we must also understand the truth found in 1 John 2:16 which says, *"For all that is in the world – the desires of the flesh and the desires of the eyes and the pride of life – is not from the Father but is from the world."* Every human heart is also born into sin and the sin nature within every single person contains these three things mentioned in 1 John. Another way to look at each of these from a childlike perspective is that we all develop a dream of the person we want to BE (pride of life), the things we want to DO (lust of the flesh), and the results we want to HAVE (lust of the eyes). The beauty and mystery that God places within our hearts is quickly controlled by our sin nature and creates the dreams we have as young children. We believe that the realization of these dreams will ultimately provide us with the significance and security we need – we believe it will make us who we are "supposed to be."

Only after the dreams to BEing, DOing, and HAVing are formed does pain enter the picture in a child's life. You can see in the diagram the arrow coming in from the left labeled Fear and Pain. You can also see the other arrows penetrating the heart representing the pain you have endured because of dreams unrealized and hurtful words received. Pain comes to children in many different forms, but it always hits the heart. The pain is only hurtful because it comes from someone in your life upon whom you have placed the highest levels of significance. Often it will come from the father.

The role of the father was established by God to be the one responsible for pointing the children and family to God. In the eyes of children, the father instinctively holds the place of highest significance. If your father was absent or less significant, the pain in your life could also have come from your mother, brother, sister, aunt, uncle, grandparent, or friends. Regardless of who inflicted the pain, it is critically important that you avoid taking on the role of a victim because of this pain.

The people who have hurt you the most likely did so inadvertently and often with the greatest intentions. Many fathers hurt their children inadvertently in an effort to make them more useful to society and better equipped for life. Instead of encouraging the beauty and mystery as God placed it in their sons or daughters, many fathers set out to recreate images of themselves in their children and fall drastically short of what God intended for their children's lives. A father who played football all his life may put that expectation on his son, even though God created his son to be an artist. The father may inflict wounds in his son's heart because he doesn't know any better. This father's significance and security now rest on whether his son will be able to represent the family well as a football player. You can see how the cycle of the wounded heart is passed on from generation to generation.

Again, the real enemy isn't the person who hurt you, but rather it is the one who orchestrated the pain and that is our adversary, the devil. The person who hurt you was the vessel for the heart attack which was perfected generations before you arrived. There is a long line of hurt people that create generational sin. Instead of seeing yourself as a victim, you need to have compassion for those who have hurt you as they themselves have also been hurt. It isn't who hurt you, or how they hurt you that we will be dealing with in the remainder of this book, but rather what you did with the pain. Once you took matters into your own hands to deal with the pain you became responsible before God. Dealing with pain through the world's system results in sin and creates the strongholds that you will root out of your life as you come to Jesus for the truth and healing.

Think back on your childhood dreams of who you wanted to BE, what you wanted to DO, and what you hoped to HAVE as a result. The person who caused you the first significant pain is the one who stepped between you and the realization of those dreams. One of the young men I counseled shared with me his dreams as a young child of what he wanted to be, what he wanted to do, and what he hoped to have. Sharing those dreams in your own life will be your practical assignment in chapter 4, and touching on this now will help you process your memories as you head that direction.

The young man's dream was to <u>be</u> a husband and father because he believed his father held the most significant position in life. Watching his father lead his mother and the children was the beauty and mystery this young man desired in his heart. He realized that what he wanted to <u>do</u> was to rescue a beautiful bride and have children with her, again seeing that as obtaining the greatest level of significance in his own life. And this young man realized that what he wanted to <u>have</u> was the love that his beautiful bride and children would give him, which would be the greatest level of security he believed to be possible.

31

However, this young man's pain entered his heart as the result of his own father jokingly pointing out his son's small physical stature. Each time the young man's physical size was joked about he felt the realization of his dream being pushed further and further away, until finally he believed the lie that his size would prevent him from rescuing any bride. Another painful arrow hit this young man's heart when his inability to learn in school like other kids was pointed out by his mother. Today this man is dealing with an addiction to pornography as a result of trying to deal with the pain through the world's system. He now believes lies about himself because of inadvertent comments from his parents. The lies he believes are preventing him from realizing the significance and security he can experience in a relationship with God. These lies rest in his heart and have become the guide for his behavior – until he realizes they are lies, renounces them, and replaces them with the truth his behavior will continue.

In the diagram these lies are represented on the arrows penetrating the heart by the words "core lies" which comes from David Clarke's book *6 Steps to Emotional Freedom*.[ii] Some of the assignments you will complete throughout this book come from the process Clarke outlines in his book. These core lies have the opportunity to take root in children because children who are not trained in the way they should go (Deuteronomy 6:4-6) do not understand that significance and security can only come from the heavenly Father. All children are born believing significance and security come from achieving the right formula of BEing, DOing, and HAVing – but these only come from the world (1 John 2:16).

The arrows in the diagram representing pain are broken because children learn at a very young age to cope with the pain they encounter. Many psychologists have looked at this in a positive light, but if we understand the Bible we will see how dangerous this can be for children. Douglas Davies refers to the Middle Childhood Development period as the ages of 5-8 years old when children begin to utilize their cognitive thinking to satiate their perceived needs.[iii] The ability for children to cope with the pain creates the necessity for the child to find a protective mechanism to avoid future encounters with the perceived source of the original pain. The child's self-protection takes the form of coping mechanisms which are represented by the circle around the heart of "ME" in the diagram.

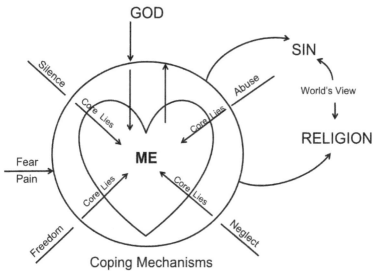

Coping mechanisms are a child's best attempt to use psychological or physical satiation to numb or avoid possible pain. The circle is drawn through the arrows to indicate the attempt to block out the possibility of future pain which is actually fear. The problem is that even though children think that the coping mechanism is protection, the original pain still arrived at the heart which formed the core lies that began to affect their behavior. Coping mechanisms also create a devastating result by closing off the heart to the love offered by the Father which is represented by the broken arrow from God. People who have experienced pain and developed coping mechanisms have only <u>thought</u> they found a way to avoid pain, but in reality have only created a pattern of behavior that is far more damaging than the original pain.

As I struggled with my own addictions I would often feel a void in my soul – I couldn't really tell if I was lonely, hungry, tired, or just depressed, but I simply felt like something was missing. The Father eventually helped me to realize that the void was simply His beckoning for a deeper relationship with me. We mistake this loving spiritual call for a potential pain and we quickly push it away through the use of our coping mechanisms. This realization was a turning point in my life and I hope it is for you as well. When I realized that God was using these moments to call out to me, I simply stopped trying to cope in those times, and I embraced the voids I felt by waiting on Him to fill me. Every time I waited He was faithful to meet me and carry me into a closer relationship with Himself.

Your captivity today is a result of the pain you experienced and the coping mechanisms you developed based on the core lies you believe. You may have more than one coping mechanism and you may adjust them when one is not appropriate in any given setting. It is critical that you make the connection between coping mechanisms and addiction. Once a child discovers a coping mechanism that gives them the greatest feeling of transcendence or "high", they will return to it again and again every time a perceived pain is approaching, and thus becoming an addict to its temporary sensation.

Transcendence is the sensation in your total being that you have just experienced something much bigger and much more fulfilling than yourself. Once the coping mechanism is firmly established and the addiction is rooted in your life you can say that your heart is trapped. Instead of finding true significance and security God's way, the heart is only capable of feeling as good as it can with the coping mechanism/addiction it has chosen. A false transcendence is created and relied upon only solidifying the trap around the heart.

The world's view of our lives is often only through the evidence of our external actions that people can see. The diagram shows this view to the right and is seen in one of two forms, sin or religion – both involve only external behavior. A problem we face today in the church at large is many are only dealing with behaviors instead of peoples' hearts. The external behavior in a person's life is only the symptom of the disease in the heart. If God deals with the heart of man, the church also ought to deal with the heart of man.

As you can see, there is far more going on under the surface in your life than you may have realized. Addressing each of these areas in your own life will show the Lord your willingness to obey and your desire to be set free. God's desire to free you is greater than your desire to be free. Trust Him that even now He is guiding you toward a peace and contentment you never thought possible. How can we teach people to obey the greatest commandment to love if we don't first work to set their hearts free?

The Original Core Lie

The reason we all seek ways to become significant and secure even from our youngest years is because we are created with needs. Dr. Larry Crabb makes the statement, "Since God is an infinite and personal being it follows that man made in His image is a finite and personal being. As a finite being, he is dependent on external resources to meet his needs: he is a contingent being."[iv]   Every human is created with needs that cannot be met on their own; however, man in his sin nature believes that through being, doing, and having he will be able to meet his own needs. This is exactly where your heart lies today as you struggle to find freedom. Proverbs 14:12 says, *"There is a way that seems right to a man, but its end is the way to death."* To better understand man's needs and inability to meet them on our own we need to look at earth's first couple Adam and Eve.

From the very beginning, God provided man with everything they would ever need. God did not leave out one detail in meeting the needs of His creation. Genesis 2:7 says that God made man from the dust and breathed life into his body. Verse 8 says that God planted a garden in Eden and put the man in it – God provided him with a home. Verse 9 says that God provided trees that were not only good for food, but were also pleasing to the eyes which would satisfy man's appetite for beauty. Verse 10 says that God provided the water necessary for the garden. Verse 15 says that God gave Adam a job and put significance on his life by allowing him to work in the garden and keep it for God. Verse 18 tells us that God saw man alone and that it was not good, or was incomplete unlike the rest of His creation, so God decided to bring him a helper. Verses 19-20 say that God formed the beasts of the earth and gave Adam the adventure of naming them all, and yet not a helper was found suitable. Verse 22 tells us that God used the rib He took from Adam and formed woman and gave her to the man providing the security or love that marriage is designed for, which satisfied another part of man's appetite for beauty. Genesis 3:8 goes on to say that Adam and Eve heard the sound of the Lord God walking in the garden in the cool of the day. Not only did God provide the security of an earthly relationship, but far greater, He provided the security of a heavenly relationship with man by spending time with them in the garden.

Out of this perfect creation God also met all the needs of the woman. While giving Eve the purpose of sharing in the work of Adam as a helpmeet, God also satisfied woman with the security of having a head, her husband. Eve was immediately provided both significance and security following her creation. She also experienced an intimate and transcendent relationship with the Lord God, which made her part of something much bigger than herself. It was in this perfect place, where all their needs were met with perfect beauty and mystery, perfect significance and security, and perfect transcendence with God that the enemy came to offer doubt.

Satan came, as we know, in the form of a serpent and presented doubt through his questions. He was able to convince man that perfection wasn't good enough, and that they needed to take things into their own hands so that more could be achieved. At the root of every trapped heart sits this very same lie – that God is not enough. Man was convinced that God had held out on them and they took the fruit from the tree they were instructed not to touch. As soon as they did, sin entered the world and the desire to BE, DO, and HAVE entered human nature, bringing the curse of original sin. The lust of the flesh, the lust of the eyes, and the pride of life are all linked to the original core lie; there must be more!

Your problem at its source is tied to this lie. Your individual core lies will be specifically unique to your life, but you will have the underlying lie that God is not enough to meet your needs and provide you with the beauty and mystery that brings

37

contentment. Because you believe that He is not enough you constantly reach for the right formula of BEing, DOing, and HAVing to appease your appetite for more.

The Hierarchy of Needs

God chose to create us as finite beings with needs. These needs can be listed and arranged in a hierarchy so that we better understand them in light of our own existence. You will notice that this list is directly parallel to the needs God met – in order – for Adam and Eve. Abraham Maslow is credited with the arrangement of these needs, when in reality God established our needs and also the meeting of our needs with the first people He ever created. But by looking at Maslow's Hierarchy of Needs[v] you can personalize these needs in your own life.

This hierarchy of needs when first established was limited to 5 levels of needs, the first four are deficiency needs, and the last need is a growth need. A "deficiency need" simply means that when the need is not met, no other needs are important and the individual will continue to put all effort into having the lowest level deficiency need met before moving on to the next need level. The hierarchy looks like this:

1. Physiological needs – the need for food and water.
2. Safety needs – that if a person has food and water, there is a need to know that there will be food and water for tomorrow. This is the need for protection.
3. Security – or the need for love – something that can only be received through interaction with others.
4. Significance – or purpose, which again can only be received through interaction with others.

5. <u>Self-actualization</u> – Maslow describes this need as the development of oneself into a full, creative, self-expressing person – your self-worth, the only level where transcendence is possible.

The critical point of this research is to see how it holds up to the truth of the Bible and how it also applies in your own heart. So let's see what the Bible says about these needs:

1. Physiological needs – Matthew 6:25 *"Therefore I tell you, do not worry about your life, what you will eat or drink, or about your body, what you will wear...32 and your heavenly Father knows that you need them...33 But seek first His kingdom and His righteousness, and all these things will be given to you as well."*

2. Safety needs – Matthew 6:34 *"Therefore do not worry about tomorrow..."* Philippians 4:19 *"And my God will meet all your needs according to His glorious riches in Christ Jesus."*

3. Security (Love) need – Romans 8:35 *"Who shall separate us from the love of Christ?"* Romans 5:8 *"But God demonstrated His own love for us in this: while we were still sinners, Christ died for us."*

4. Significance (Purpose) need – Philippians 1:21 *"For me, to live is Christ and to die is gain."* Ephesians 2:10 *"For we are God's workmanship, created in Christ Jesus to do good works, which God prepared in advance for us to do."*

5. Self-actualization (Transcendence) need – Ecclesiastes 3:11 *"He has made everything beautiful in its time. He has also set eternity in the hearts of men; yet they cannot fathom what God has done from beginning to end."*

These verses represent some of the promises of God for the meeting of all our needs – but what happens when we take God out of the picture and we are left on our own to figure out how our needs will be met? We set out as children to meet our own needs under our own power and abilities before we are introduced to God's plan. Meeting your own needs through self-reliance results in the formation of the trapped heart.

Removing God

What does it look like when you remove God's promises from this hierarchy of needs? Removing God's promises and the awareness of His ability to meet needs results in people who fend for themselves. Babies cry and fuss when their physiological needs are not being met – parents feed them, and eventually a toddler is able to feed himself after watching mom gather food around the kitchen. A similar experience is found in the second level need, a child that is scared or fearful about what the night might bring or what tomorrow might bring, may learn to cope with those feelings by creating a place where they feel safe – under the covers, under the bed, in mom and dad's bed, or in the closet, etc. In essence, the need on the first two levels can be partially met by the individual alone – although ultimately God is the One who meets all of our needs.

The major problem occurs within the needs found in the next two levels of Maslow's hierarchy. Trying to satisfy the deficit of security and significance requires interaction with other people. Created for relationship with God, and with other people, we are incapable of meeting the needs for security and significance in and of ourselves. Because these two need levels fall within the category of deficiency needs, people often fail to reach the fifth level of self-actualization or self-worth. This fifth level is a growth need and is only possible as people feel significant and secure, or another way to say it, is that they experience genuine self-worth. Once the self-worth is experienced, the person has the need to grow in intellect and experience, or maturity. If a person never fulfills the deficit of security or significance in their heart, the result is immaturity.

Maslow determined in his research that approximately only 2% of the population achieved the fifth level need of self-actualization. That means that potentially 98% of people live their entire lives searching for significance and security in this life, trying to achieve it through their own devised means. The means of self-gratification, as we know, become their coping mechanisms and continually leave them short of reaching true self-worth.

The greater the pain you felt as a child the better you had to get at coping with the pain. The scars that resulted in your life are associated with the pain, and the pain is associated with the circumstances that brought it about. The amazing thing about the metaphysical makeup of our life is how well it can attune itself to recognizing when the potential for similar pain may be encountered. This means that any time you sense the potential for pain you are quick to utilize your coping mechanisms that you have perfected, in order to avoid the pain by trying to help

41

yourself feel better. Are you able to identify in your own life what these primary coping mechanisms are? If so, begin to write them down in your journal.

God Alone

Since the fall in the Garden of Eden, man on his own is unable to experience the kind of intimacy God designed because perfection cannot dwell with imperfection. The deficit that we feel is designed to draw us toward God and to choose that intimacy with Him through faith in the provision of His Son, Jesus Christ. A relationship with God through Jesus Christ is salvation. It is a gift given by the grace of God. By believing that Jesus is who He said He is, and did what He said He did, and by recognizing that you are totally incapable of gaining a relationship with God apart from Him, God saves you by His grace. True belief in Jesus is marked by repentance, which is the turning away from your sin. God saves you by His grace and places you into His Son, Jesus Christ. No longer does God look at you, the sinner, but He looks at Jesus Christ – your advocate and defender (1 John 2:1-2). God uses this deficit within us to draw us to Himself. As we will learn, He uses our relationships with other people, guided by His control, to meet the needs He created within us. You must see Him as the source for meeting all your needs.

Satisfying the deficit of security and significance in your life will only come through a real love relationship with Jesus Christ. As you learn to love through the practical steps in this book you will be maturing in love. 1 Corinthians 13:11 says, *"When I was a child, I spoke like a child, I thought like a child, I reasoned like a child. When I became a man, I gave up childish ways."* Only true love with God can help us put away our childish ways. The addiction or coping mechanism you face is a childish way of trying to meet your own deficit of security and significance. Now that you have identified the problem, the source, the needs, and the answer, you can take steps toward seeing these childish ways depart from your life.

Write this verse down in the front of your journal and review it every day and read through it as you continue on this journey toward your Genesis Moment. 1 John 4:18, *"There is no fear in love. But perfect love drives out fear, because fear has to do with punishment. The one who fears is not made perfect in love."* The fear of being hurt is keeping you from true love. The only way you will find freedom is to find love, and the only way to love is through your willingness to possibly be hurt. There is no reward without risk – the beautiful truth of God's word is His faithfulness to love you through those risky moments – He simply wants you to trust Him and obey.

If you are someone who is deeply entrenched in an addiction and feeling hopeless even after reading through these first chapters I want you to at least acknowledge something with me before you move on. Acknowledge out loud that your addiction is not eternal.

Say this, "My addiction is not eternal. It will end." You will never see the idea of an eternal addiction even once in the Bible – the adage "once an addict always an addict" is a lie Satan uses to keep people in captivity. Instead, the Bible promises that through compassionate obedience any chain, any addiction, and any bondage will be destroyed by the power of Jesus Christ. I pray that you understand the source of your problem, and rather than listening to the enemy who is telling you that you are too evil, too dirty, or too far gone, you will hear the Lord say that you are just like everyone else in this world. As long as you have breath in your lungs you have a chance to humble yourself and see His mighty power at work in your life.

Moving from darkness into the light is going to be a different process for each person. Just like creation, God is creating new life in you and you will move at the pace He has determined. In the next chapter we will look at the move from darkness into light and see what instruction the Bible offers in leading us one step closer to your Genesis Moment.

Reflections:

1. List specifically again which of your struggles are coping mechanisms and try and order them from strongest to weakest as it relates to their control of your behavior.

2. As you reflect on beauty and mystery as you see it, can you write down some things that you find to be beautiful and mysterious? In a brief summary, how do those things relate to your passions which God created in you?

3. Believing is critical to understanding – reflect on the struggles you have been facing and settle in your heart that Jesus is able to free you from these struggles. In a few bullet points write down some Scriptures or ideas that stood out to you from this chapter about the promises of God and meditate upon them.

Chapter 3

From Dark to Light

Often when a person is walking in darkness they are unaware of the darkness in which they exist. The only way darkness can be revealed is through light. If you have truly believed in Jesus and entered into a relationship with Him based on faith, then you now know the difference between the darkness and the light. Every believer's salvation experience is unique because God does not follow a formula. God's creative work of speaking light from the darkness, as He did on the first day of creation, is unique in each soul He brings to life.

Regardless of how or when you were saved, your story is now a tool for you to use in sharing the power of Jesus with others. Your unique life circumstances have shaped you into you, and now you have a history that relates to people who have also lived a similar life to you. Don't fail to use your life as evidence of the power of God to save and deliver. I was personally brought to a "now or never" decision myself after a life of thinking I was already a Christian.

Hearing about how John the Baptist prepared the way for Jesus one morning in church, the Holy Spirit suddenly brought me an awareness of my own sin. I sensed the Holy Spirit telling me that the life I had been living was leading many people toward an eternity in hell. At that moment, He was giving me faith to step into a relationship with Christ who would use my life to draw men to Himself. The decision I had to make was being challenged by the enemy who was trying to convince me that I was already saved. You see, when you walk in darkness, believing that you are walking in light, you are walking in the most dangerous darkness a soul can experience. I walked in arrogance for many years regarding my perceived light. However, that day, the Lord made it clear that I was not walking in the light, but was in fact lost in the darkness.

I use this to illustrate the importance of a humble perspective of your own life. This principle is critical to understanding how your coping mechanisms and struggles are truly more powerful than you may care to admit. Often people don't want to admit how dark their life has really become. Our society holds people to an external standard which creates an unhealthy expectation of maintaining an image acceptable to their circles of influence. The reality is, your healing and your progress is completely dependent upon your ability to be real, and your commitment to admit the truth regardless of your appearance.

"Then you will know the truth, and the truth will set you free." John 8:32

Providence

It is not a coincidence that you find yourself reading this book today. It is not a coincidence that you have lived a life that has brought you to a place of needing help to relieve the ache in your heart. There are no coincidences in this life. There are many things that happen on a daily basis that are seemingly out of our control. However, each and every one of the circumstances we have been a part of have been allowed through the sovereign hands of God. Isaiah 46:10 says, *"declaring the end from the beginning and from ancient times things not yet done, saying, 'My counsel shall stand, and I will accomplish all my purpose.'"*

I have heard many people say, "I wish I would have learned this years ago," or "I have wasted so much time." As you draw closer to your own Genesis Moment you need to remove these kinds of thoughts from your mind. God in His providence is accomplishing His will despite our abilities or inabilities. You are being brought to a new place in your life at just the right time to fulfill the purpose God has already declared. On this side of heaven we will never be able to completely thank God for the fact of His sovereign control over all things. Only when we see Him face to face will we realize how His provision, protection, and position held us in His grip.

As you continue to walk through each of these chapters you need to pay attention to the providence of God. One of the ways God speaks to His people is through themes. It is critical that you are either reading or listening to the Word of God daily. The reason this is critical is because the Word does not return void. Many people who have not yet built a genuine love for Christ have difficulty reading or appreciating the Scriptures. However, by faith, if you will read the Word or listen to the Word each day you will find that themes will appear in what you hear and read.

A theme may appear as you pick out some Bible passages each day over the course of a few days, and it seems that each of them reference forgiveness. This would be God using His Word, which is living and active, to bring you under conviction. If you realize that He keeps bringing up forgiveness, then you know you need to forgive someone. Don't delay that obedience, through His providence He has allowed you an opportunity to draw near to Him through the obedience of forgiveness. (this may be one of those moments He is using in that theme for you) The themes will continue and will change over time, but without the Word going in, the power for change is impossible.

One other way you will pick up on these themes that God illuminates in your life, is through listening to multiple preachers on a weekly basis. Maybe you have the ability to listen to Godly men preaching on the radio each day. Today with the internet you are able to listen to any number of sermons that have been recorded and uploaded in various places. What you will find is that God uses these men and women who teach His Word to also providentially lead you to a specific area or theme that God wants to deal with in your life. This is why Hebrews 10:25 commands us not to forsake the assembling of ourselves together, but to stir each other up to love and good deeds.

I see some of you rolling your eyes and allowing those past feelings toward the Bible to cloud over you right now. You need to stop those feelings. You may not have ever appreciated the Bible before, but if you believe that Jesus has the power to save you, then you must believe He has the power to give you a love for His Word. He said in Psalm 132 that He elevates His Word above His name. As you move forward in the Bible by faith, you can be assured that God will reward you with understanding, and not just understanding but with a passion for His Word.

Salvation means that the Spirit of God is placed within you. The Spirit of God loves the Word; therefore, you will also grow to love the Word.

The Work

There are many people today claiming to have a saving relationship with Jesus who have never genuinely repented. The real work of walking with Jesus is actually turning away from sin and self, and relying on faith to obey His commands. No one ever said salvation was easy. In fact Jesus taught more than one parable about counting the cost before beginning to build, and understanding the battle before going to war. But anything worth having comes through challenge.

I want to introduce you to a concept that I recognized in my own life that I called "selfish safety." The fear that rose up once I had committed my life to Christ, was the fear of giving up the things I enjoyed. The initial feeling for a new Christian is one of losing all the fun out of life, but this is also a tactic of the enemy. While you walk in darkness, you are a slave to sin (Rom 6:20). As a slave to sin, everything you do is sin and is rooted in pleasing self. This is why your coping mechanisms were formed. But selfish safety comes into a new Christian's life because they feel safer doing the things they always did while walking in darkness rather than giving them up. You would rather please yourself in some way, than even think about not knowing what you would do if you suddenly had that void in your life.

Germans call this fear, angst. It is a fear of the unknown. Selfish safety causes you to think that if you give up those things you do, even though you know how bad they are, you won't have anything to enjoy. This is also a lie of Satan's kingdom. Remember the verse I gave you in the 2nd chapter which says we are not given a spirit of fear from God? Therefore, you have to overcome selfish safety in your own life and give up the sinful ways you have been pleasing yourself with if indeed you want to walk in this relationship with Jesus.

Obviously the reason for writing this book is because some of those sinful patterns are not going to disappear overnight. Still, you will need to continue faithfully with the desire to see them relinquished in your life. The hard work begins with confession. Openly confessing your sin is the way for healing to come into your heart (James 5:16). We will look deeper into confession as we progress.

There will be results from sin that you have come to enjoy, though they have continually left you empty. The Bible says that not even a little bit of sin is acceptable to God. In fact, no sin can even exist in His presence. He commands His children to be holy because He is holy (Leviticus 19:2, I Peter 1:16).

Because confession will be critical for you as you move toward your Genesis Moment, you need to find a trusted friend who will allow you to confess your sin as it becomes evident. The concern for each believer is not whether or not they fall, but if they are willing to get back up. Proverbs 24:16 says, *"for the righteous falls seven times and rises again, but the wicked stumble in times of calamity."* This truly is the picture of God's grace, proving that He doesn't base His work on our acts of righteousness, but rather on His own Son, Jesus Christ, in our place (1 John 2:1-2).

Discipline

The Lord is faithful to discipline the sons and daughters He loves. Just read Hebrews 12 and you will find His clarity on the matter of discipline and love. No one enjoys discipline while it is being endured, but afterward it will produce a harvest of righteousness. As you press into the Lord one of the blessings He will provide you is the awareness of your sin. As this awareness is realized your first response will be to resist. This is our carnal nature's first response to the Spirit's conviction. There may be periods of weeks or even months where this resistance to a conviction God has given will remain in control. However, eventually through the love of Christ, He will provide enough pressure that eventually you will submit to His will and repent. At that moment healing takes place supernaturally. It is the miracle of God's sanctification.

Because most of your life is lived in rebellion against God, humility is a foreign concept. Humility is the outcome of discipline in the life of every Christian. The only Man who lived the perfectly humble life is Jesus Christ. Because we are to be conformed to His image this will also be an ever increasing mark for the true believer. Humility will give you an honest perspective of your own life. God disciplines to reveal the areas of your life that you are still holding back from God's control. A rebel's natural reaction is to turn away from correction. The Lord will bring visibility to these areas that have been concealed, and then He will bring correction. It will be critical for you to face the correction willingly, quickly, and faithfully.

Any time the Lord brings conviction in your heart regarding an area where sin is present you need to agree with Him about what it really is. That agreement is the definition for the word "confess" in 1 John 1:9. And if you confess your sins He is faithful and just to forgive your sins and cleanse you from all unrighteousness. If you are serious about experiencing a Genesis Moment in your life and finding true freedom it will only come through His cleansing. Whatever you do, do not turn away from His correction because when you do the Bible says that your heart will be hardened. This is how your heart was trapped in the first place. Hebrews 3 will give you greater insight into the results of not believing and obeying God and the consequences for those who refuse His correction.

God's pace and method for dealing with each hidden area of darkness in your heart will be as unique as you are. There is no formula to His sanctification, just as there is no formula to His creative power. I share this with you to encourage you because no one knows you better than the Father. He will not overwhelm you to the point of breaking you. He will not put loads upon you that will snuff out the ember that is still smoldering inside you. He has promised in Matthew 12:20 *"a bruised reed he will not break, and a smoldering wick he will not quench..."* Many times you can compare the life of the believer who is truly being sanctified to a rubber band. A rubber band will stretch a long way, but at some point the stretching will cause a break. Only God knows just how much stretch you can take before breaking. You will often think that you are at your breaking point, long before you actually are. You can trust God that He will not break you or snuff you out.

God's discipline toward humans can also be often misunderstood. Human beings interact with one another on the carnal level more than the spiritual level. Often children are punished for wrong doing, meaning they receive the penalty that is due in correlation with the offense that is committed. Children can also be abused when the penalty far exceeds the offense or a penalty is administered without an offense. God's discipline is not the same as what people call punishment. We all have to understand that the penalty we deserve for the least of our offenses is death.

Knowing that Jesus took our penalty upon Himself at the cross, we know that He atoned for our punishment and we will forever be viewed by God as justified in Christ's blood. God looks upon us, not as deserving punishment, but as needing correction and purification. God's discipline then is not punishment; it is training that creates the opportunity for us to cooperate with Him in repentance and confession for the transformation of our hearts. Always remember that God only disciplines the ones He loves. If you are not receiving regular discipline, you are an illegitimate son or daughter according to God's Word in Hebrews 12. Do not be deceived God will not be mocked and there are consequences for every believer who chooses to sin.

Receive God's discipline in your life and meet it with repentance. The sooner you learn how unable you are to change yourself the sooner you will get out of those seasons of discipline. What once took you a month to overcome will soon be down to days, and even hours as you learn to recognize God's loving transformation of your heart.

Sexual Sin

One of the most prominent areas of darkness that needs to be overcome in the lives of many believers who feel trapped and unable to escape their burden is the area of sexual sin. Though I have encountered some men and women who have not had a struggle in this area of life, they are very few and far between. One of the reasons for sexual sin to be such a stronghold is because it is essential in our obedience to God's command. God said in Genesis 2 that man was to leave father and mother and be joined to his wife as one flesh. The command to both man and woman was to be fruitful and multiply. God not only created sex, but He commanded sex, and He made sex enjoyable.

As with any other portion of God's creation, our adversary quickly works to pervert what God makes good. One thing that will help us understand the war that occurs against the sexuality of our children and our society today is the fact that angels do not procreate. Satan then is neither man nor woman, He is described with a male name and referenced in the masculine, but is not able to reproduce. The Bible also tells us that Satan is an angel of light in 2 Corinthians 11:14. If we understand this about Satan we will understand why he has fought so hard against sexuality. He hates the things he himself is unable to accomplish. He hates God because he was not able to take away God's throne. He hates man because God made us in His image. He hates sexuality because when obeyed by man in the correct way it affords the opportunity for more sons and daughters of God to be born.

Are you starting to understand why Satan's agenda aligns so closely with the homosexual and abortion agenda we see waging war against Christianity in our society? By turning sex into a method for pleasure alone, Satan is able to pervert the real intention for which God created it and to get man to walk away from God's plan. The attack on sexuality is not only limited to the homosexual community. The attack is just as strong on the heterosexual community. In all cases sexuality has been attacked and unfortunately for many people the results of the attack have led to some devastating addictions.

I am aware that you may be reading this book because you are struggling specifically with a homosexual urge or lifestyle that you have kept secret because you know it is leading you away from God. I want you to know that regardless of your struggles, Jesus has paid the penalty for all men, and He has promised freedom to all men. I hope you will be encouraged that as long as you continue to have a desire to be free from the burden you are carrying, Jesus offers you a way out. Jesus says in John 16:33 that He has overcome the world. That means He has overcome all of our problems, no matter how big they may seem.

As we have already learned in a previous chapter, all humans have needs that come from being created as finite beings and being unable to meet those needs. We are created for relationship. One of the ways God meets our needs is through other people. Sexuality is the method by which two people who are separate can become one flesh. In essence sexuality is limited in God's kingdom to a relationship. What the world has done with sex is to open it up to everyone by every method to obtain the euphoric feeling it can produce simply for the sake of the euphoric feeling. If this was the intention of sex and the reason for its creation, wouldn't the euphoric feeling produce a sense of satisfaction? And yet, for every man or woman, the euphoric feeling only results in wishing for more euphoric feelings. This is also why sexual sin is progressive.

Sexuality is sacred. One of the arguments I have heard regarding the homosexual agenda is defending their so called "civil rights". Civil rights are only possible for that which is sacred. By tying homosexuality to the oppression of the black community in America they are trying to connect both on the same level. The reason this is not possible is because race is sacred. God determines someone's race; it is not determined by man, and therefore all men are created equal and all races should be given equal rights. Much like race, sexuality is also sacred. God determines sexuality, not man. Therefore all men and women are created equally as either man or woman and must be governed as such. Choosing to step outside the sacred for the sake of pleasure does not equate to a civil right.

Ephesians 4:22 says, *"to put off your old self, which belongs to your former manner of life and is corrupt through deceitful desires,"* The way of the world is to convince men and women that the desire for sexual fulfillment is a legitimate desire. If you believe that the desire for the euphoric feeling is a legitimate desire you believe a lie. This would be the definition of a deceitful desire. If you believe that sexual intercourse sourced in serving your spouse is a legitimate desire then you would be correct. Marriage is not a license to please yourself through sexual intercourse. Many marriages today have one or both spouses still experiencing the deceitful desires of sex for pleasure in their marriage. Hebrews 13:4 says, *"Let marriage be held in honor among all, and let the marriage bed be undefiled, for God will judge the sexually immoral and adulterous."* This command does not just apply to premarital purity, but also to post marital purity.

Sexual sin is the result of believing lies about the feelings and reasons surrounding sex as created and ordained by God. When you begin to experience sexual fulfillment outside of the boundaries He established, it takes hold of your life and creates within you a craving for that "high" we talked about in the first chapter. The "high" is not enough to sustain you for any period of time, and so you being to act out more frequently and you begin to view everyone from the perspective of fulfilling your sexual desire. This is why you can walk through a mall today or even a church building and see all the men trying to look the women over and determine how "hot" they are. This is also why you will see the women dressing in such a way to get the men to turn and look them up and down.

For many women the sexual encounter with a man doesn't only translate into a euphoric feeling, it also connects them emotionally to that person and gives them a false sense of security. Because women and men are wired differently men tend to find greater significance through the conquest of sex, whereas women on the other hand tend to find greater security through the offering up of sex. These are generalizations and may apply to the majority, but there are always exceptions on both sides, especially where the homosexual community is concerned.

Men as believers in Christ who struggle with bondage to sexual sin, or sexual addiction, often do not act out frequently by having intercourse, but instead keep most of their actions concealed – things such as viewing pornography frequently and masturbating, or reaching out to various women to try and entice them into sexual exchanges of text messages or phone calls. Some men battle with frequenting the strip clubs. What you will find in each of the ways men act out their sexual addiction is that they view sex as a fulfillment of a need they have, which is actually a deceitful desire.

Women as believers who struggle with sexual addiction will also often conceal it by acting out through reading racy romance novels, watching certain television programs, and some women also battle against pornography and masturbation. Women unlike men, often look to sex as a means to obtain relational comfort. This idea that sex will provide security is also a deceitful desire.

Both men and women who struggle against this darkness in their hearts will often be led into relationships with someone who shares the same struggles. Men and women who will exchange text messages and internet exchanges often feel a "thrill" when they first begin. The exchanges bring the man a sense of significance because he is finding this woman to be interested in him. The exchanges bring the women a sense of security thinking the man may become interested enough in her to provide stability through relationship. This is a deadly combination and the results are often failed marriages because the man will not find enough significance in the woman, nor will the woman find enough security with a man who is only committed to fulfilling his own deceitful desires.

As you move from darkness to light, these places in your life revolving around sexual sin need to come into the light. It may seem taboo, and you may think that shame will be the result, but I promise that if you are faithful to confess, He is faithful and just to cleanse and comfort you. Change will not come until you have had enough of your secret life to bring it from darkness into the light and let the light wash away the darkness.

Humility

The truth of humility is found in James 4:4-8 *"You adulterous people. Do you not know that friendship with the world is enmity with God? Therefore whoever wishes to be a friend of the world makes himself an enemy of God. Or do you suppose it is to no purpose that the Scripture says, 'He yearns jealously over the spirit that he has made to dwell in us? But he gives more grace. Therefore it says, 'God opposes the proud, but gives grace to the humble.' Submit yourselves therefore to God. Resist the devil, and he will flee from you. Draw near to God, and he will draw near to you. Cleanse your hands, you sinners, and purify your hearts, you double-minded."* An adulterous person is one who is set on choosing his own sin patterns over his relationship with Jesus.

God does not desire to heal you so that you can keep your worldly lifestyle and just be free from the consequences of your sin. God heals and frees men so they can leave the worldly life behind and become vessels of honorable use in God's kingdom. Many of the people I counsel are seeking to avoid the consequences of their sin instead of actually seeking deeper intimacy with God. People may say with their words that they want to be free from sin, but soon their actions show they would rather be friends with the world than intimate with God. The freedom that exists in Christ rests wholly on the desire to be submersed in Christ and to depart from the world. Jesus desires a deep intimacy with His Bride as James says "He yearns jealously." God is yearning jealously over the spirit he placed in you right now. As a jealous lover God tells you how you can draw near to Him and it is only through humility.

As you look back at your struggle with your coping mechanisms, the way to be humble is to bring to light the works of darkness in your life. It is a humbling thing to sit in front of a brother or sister and be honest about the sin you struggle with. Once you have spoken the struggles aloud, you can never go back to the person you're talking to and say "I was only kidding." Once another person hears the truth about your life, you have committed to your admission of guilt. This is why God tells us in James 5:16 that we will be healed. Many times our confessions are only spoken to God, but, in reality He already knows our actions, and more importantly, He knows our hearts. A confession to another person shows your desire for humility and your desire to draw near to God, knowing by faith He will draw near to you.

The humility of confession was something the Lord introduced me to through a providential circumstance. God had put a man named Aaron in my life over an 8 month period of time who continually came to me asking for things he needed. Jesus had reminded me of the command to provide for others as though

59

I was providing it to Christ. He asked me to take literally His Word in Luke 6:30 that tells us to give to everyone who asks of you. There were times that friends would tell me to stop giving to Aaron because he was using me. My giving continued even at times that it made no sense to me. But as I gave, God would bless me by making another area of my darkness (sin) visible so that I could confess and the humility of openly confessing that sin brought great healing to my life. All of this was occurring before I ever experienced my Genesis Moment. And today God still desires my obedience in giving, and He still requires my obedience to confess openly the sins He reveals.

James 3:2 says, *"For we all stumble in many ways. And if anyone does not stumble in what he says, he is a perfect man, able also to bridle his whole body."* Stumbling is far different than coping. Through your own obedience and humility you will continue to experience a deeper relationship with Jesus Christ.

If you are serious about experiencing freedom, ask Jesus to give you His humility by the power of His Spirit. He will work humility into your life as you obey His Word. I have drawn a diagram that represents the acts of compassionate obedience it will take in your life to see this healing come forth. The diagram looks like this.

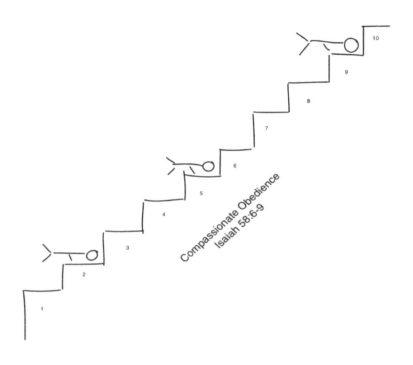

Each stair represents an act of compassionate obedience that the Lord will provide. Step one for me was represented by Aaron showing up on my doorstep that night looking for money for his electric bill. The staircase is not consistent because the Lord will continue to provide you with opportunities that will not all be the same. Some of the opportunities He provides will be extremely inconvenient – a ride for someone at midnight when you would rather sleep. And some will be simpler – buying someone a meal or coffee in line because God placed them on your heart. Regardless of what God presents you with, the key is to remain faithful in serving others. The key to your Genesis Moment is found in Isaiah 58:6-7 which says *"Is not this the fast*

that I choose: to loose the bonds of wickedness, to undo the straps of the yoke, to let the oppressed free, and to break every yoke? Is it not to share your bread with the hungry and bring the homeless poor into your house; when you see the naked, to cover him, and not to hide yourself from your own flesh?"

This staircase represents those acts of compassion the Lord has chosen to use to bring you into freedom. The image of the man face down on three of those steps represents you and me. As we walk with the Lord in obedience, we may fall or stumble as James says. The key to falling is what Solomon said in Proverbs 24:16 *"for the righteous falls seven times and rises again, but the wicked stumble in times of calamity."* We must learn of God's grace in such a way that when we do fall, we confess to a brother or sister, stand up, and take the next step of compassionate obedience presented to us by the Lord.

When David had sinned against the Lord with Bathsheba God sent Nathan to rebuke him. When David realized his sin against God he said in 2 Samuel 12:13 *"David said to Nathan, 'I have sinned against the Lord.' And Nathan said to David, 'The Lord also has put away your sin; you shall not die.'"* The grace of God is that we must stand on His righteousness, not our own, and understand that we were forgiven when Jesus was crucified. We must not continue in sin that grace may abound, but when we fall, we must rise in confession and take the next step.

The enemy does not want you to stand up on stair #2 and proceed to #3, he wants you to lie there defeated in your guilt, ineffective as God's vessel. Always remember that you must believe the Lord will give you the power to rise and continue. The enemy also wants you to think that all the ground gained is lost – too many people think that falling puts them back at ground zero. The truth is God's ground can never be lost – what He starts He finishes. As you take those next steps you will see that there is a longer distance between falls. Though you fell once in two steps, you may only fall twice in five or three times in 15. The point is not to keep track of acts of compassionate obedience and the number of times you fall, but that you must walk up the stairs in a lifestyle of serving others, confessing your sin, standing up under God's grace, and taking the next step closer to God. It is a staircase we never stop climbing! James tells us *"Draw near unto God and He will draw near unto you."* The responsibility you have is to remain humble and useable in the hands of God. You can trust Him to make a way.

The Resources

There were two significant sources of encouragement that I want to share with you that helped me through the healing process. The first is a book by David Clarke, *Six Steps to Emotional Freedom.*[vi] As a licensed counselor and psychologist, David truly helps people understand that their addictions and struggles are not unexplainable but are the result of emotional pain. This is something we will continue to examine through the course of this book.

The second critical source of encouragement is a book by John Eldredge and Brent Curtis call *Sacred Romance.*[vii] *Sacred Romance* helped me understand God's love for me as I had never understood it before. John and Brent share from personal experience about how God brought them both to realize His love. I don't think any of us can ever truly grasp the depths of God's love for us so any book or resource that can help us draw closer to Him is extremely valuable.

63

Freedom

You may be wondering what exactly the Genesis Moment is. The Genesis Moment is the moment when God speaks the creative word over your addiction or cyclical pattern of sin and you are instantly healed. When God spoke in Genesis 1:3 and said the word "light" there was light. When Jesus spoke "get up, take your mat and walk," there was healing. God's creative power is found in His Words and only He can speak the words of healing into your heart and in that instant you will experience your own Genesis Moment. Creation was not earned. Creation itself is an act of God's grace. Your healing is not earned; it is an act of God's grace. God's promise of freedom comes before our ability to seek Him.

Jeremiah 29:13 says, *"You will seek me and find me, when you seek me with all your heart."* You are not on a journey toward earning your freedom. You are on a journey to discover whether or not you really want to seek God with all your heart. He already knows what you will choose; you are the one who needs to find out. When God breathes His Word of healing into your life you will be filled with an understanding deep inside that something supernatural has changed your thoughts, motives, and actions.

My personal testimony of this moment came overnight. I went to sleep as a man in bondage and trapped by my coping mechanisms. I woke up the next morning with the understanding I just described and my world has never been the same since. I was suddenly immersed in my Savior's love and He was enough for me. I experienced a sense of deep contentment and peace, something I had never experienced before. It was like winning the spiritual lottery, only there was no gamble; just the gift of love as I was receiving my spiritual inheritance. It was very hard for me to believe, because like the man who couldn't walk before Jesus healed him, I could not love until Jesus healed me. I kept wondering if I would wake up from the dream or if I had somehow convinced myself, but nothing could explain away the change except the loving grace of my heavenly Father. John 8:36 says, *"So if the Son sets you free, you will be free indeed."* The Lord has truly done a miraculous work in my life and I know He is going to do a miraculous work in your life as well.

The period of time immediately following your Genesis Moment is best likened to that of a honeymoon with Jesus. You will experience a bond with the Lord and a deep love that only He could place in your heart, soul, and mind. For the first time you will come to understand what He means by His command to love God with all your heart, all your soul, all your mind, and all your strength, and to love your neighbor as yourself. None of that is possible when coping mechanisms trap your heart. His freedom shatters the prison around your heart, puts all the broken pieces back together again, and seals them with His love. Your Genesis Moment will be the creation of a heart of flesh and the destruction of a heart of stone. You will feel like you have just come through open heart surgery, and following that surgery you will need the care and protection only Jesus can provide.

Though books will be written and words will be shared, there is only one true book that provides the answer we all earnestly desire and that book is the Bible. God's Word never returns void (Isaiah 55:11), but always accomplishes what the Lord desires. He desires your freedom, do you? He is the only One who can free you and He does so by a miracle of grace and no other way. Isaiah 58:8-9 reveal this truth and say, *"Then shall your light break forth like the dawn, and your healing shall spring up speedily; your righteousness shall go before you; the glory of the Lord shall be your rear guard."* My prayer for you is that the Lord is drawing you into greater desire for Him and that you are being encouraged to go all the way.

Destination

Our enemy will work hard to take whatever good that God gives and twist it into darkness. Our responsibility is to daily submit ourselves to the Lord and to renew our minds in His word to avoid the twisting of the enemy. Some people look to experiences with God as though they will be the destination. This is one way the enemy twists good things into evil. Your Genesis Moment is not the destination; it's actually the starting point. That is why it's called a Genesis Moment. One thing the enemy will do is try to convince you to perform for the sake of achieving. But before you reach your goal he will also place major stumbling blocks in your path to try and keep you from reaching an experience with God.

In the book *Sacred Romance,* the authors speak of how the devil will present us with a perfect opportunity to grab onto the little indulgences we've enjoyed in order to keep us from tipping over into fully committing to the Lord in repentance.[viii] Because your enemy is familiar with your coping mechanisms he will work to offer you the perfect opportunity with the right person, place, and time to get you to reach for the coping mechanisms rather than reaching for Christ.

An example of this is found in John 5 when Jesus encounters a paralytic man beside the pool who has been there for many years. Jesus asks him if he wants to be healed. The man responds with excuses of why he hasn't been healed. The enemy works to remind us of the reasons why things won't work.

Despite the man's excuse, Jesus spoke the creative word over the man and he was instantly healed. He didn't need the water; he only needed Jesus' Word.

You may experience these same kinds of obstacles, excuses, reasons, people, relationships, etc. Whatever the enemy has used against you over the years you need to realize that all you need is Jesus. Do not let the enemy hold you back from your freedom by losing heart and seeking your own way – press into Jesus even when it gets tough.

We never arrive in this life. Your healing will be comparable to Jesus healing the lame man. If Jesus healed the lame man and gave him the ability to walk, but the man never got off his mat, how would he ever use his freedom? The same is true for you when Christ sets you free. He releases your captive heart so you will once again leap for joy as you are filled with love for Him. Freedom is not a destination you are trying to reach, but a gateway to the life Jesus wants you to live. Your Genesis Moment will create an addiction to holiness that will bring you back time and time again for more of the Lord's presence.

In the following chapters we are going to lay out some practical steps and homework that follow God's commands to help you experience the freedom found in your Genesis Moment. Regardless of what you are facing, the truths of God's Word will be faithful to deliver you, as long as you are willing to obey. We live in a church age where pastors are guilty of not teaching obedience as Christ commanded. We have sidelined obedience, the mortification of our sin nature, and holiness while trading them in for entertainment, comfort, and thrills. For you to experience the love and freedom that God offers there is no greater element necessary than your willingness to obey all that God commands. Somehow the idea of obedience in the church got translated into oppression, but in reality, obedience is freedom. Obedience is freedom to feel secure love, freedom to feel significant, and freedom to experience the transcendence that is only found when the presence of God is manifested intimately within you.

I hope you were brought face to face with some of your own coping mechanisms as you read this chapter. Only when you recognize your problem can you come to the Lord for His healing. Don't forget the key to intimacy with God is not found in your righteousness, but in your humility. James 4:8 tells us that God opposes the proud, but gives grace to the humble. Humility is found in the heart of the people who admit their problems and confess their sins to one another. God's true love deposited in your heart sets you free from the slavery of sin and brings you from darkness into light.

Walking in the light allows you to walk blameless before the Lord just as He commands. None of us will ever be perfect on this earth – but all of us can be blameless where there is no hidden sin or sinful motivation for the things we do. We will still stumble and fall and darkness will be revealed because of our sin nature, but the intention of the blameless person is to live in a manner worthy of the Lord, Romans 12:1-2. A blameless person has no secret life, and will confess their sins openly to another person with a humble heart; but a trapped heart will go to great measures to conceal it (Psalm 32:5). If you have made the decision in your heart to go all the way make the following prayer your own as you drop to a knee and seek the Lord.

A Prayer of Surrender

Lord, I want to praise you for being the God of all comfort, for being the only righteous ruler, for being the everlasting Father. I want to open my heart today in surrender to You Jesus. I admit that I have been trying to cope with my own deficiencies and everything I have tried has come up short. I know that I have created addictions in my life, some that I may not even see today, but I want to release them to Your control Father. Just as an earthly father knows how to give good gifts, how much more do You, my heavenly Father, know how to give good gifts, so I ask for Your gift of healing and I commit to walking obediently with You as You command. I ask for Your Spirit of courage and wisdom, the Spirit of revelation and knowledge to guide me as I give up my life to honor You and for the first time step into the love relationship You so graciously offer. I love You Lord and I thank You for my life. Not my will be done, but Yours.

Reflections:

1. In just a few summary points, how can you relate to those areas of darkness we covered? Include any memories that were brought back to you as a result of reading this chapter.

2. The ultimate core lie is "there is something more" – what are some of the core lies you can identify in your own heart? Write them down as you think of them.

3. Identify a few Scriptures that were impressed upon you through this chapter and summarize them in your own words as you meditate on what God is saying to you.

Chapter 4

Start Right Now!

As you prayed that prayer I trust the Lord is giving you a strong desire to dig into this process. The first step is looking for the opportunities to serve others in acts of compassionate obedience that He will provide. Never stop looking for ways to serve others. God will reward your obedience. Always keep the staircase of Isaiah 58:6-7 fresh in your mind.

As you have already read, the place to start is humility. The hard work of humility is to take an honest look at the person you have become and the road you took in getting here. There are many circumstances and situations that have been a part of your past that have contributed to your current condition. Just as we learned from the coping mechanism diagram, unresolved pain is the greatest influencer of your behavior today.

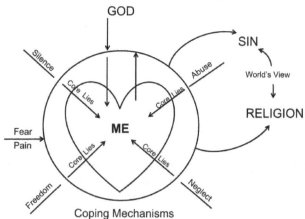

The pain that some people experience as young children is so hurtful that their heart found a way to bury the memory all together. This is how the heart sought protection. Unfortunately instead of protection, the heart hardens, developing a more powerful stronghold than the pain. The Lord desires to take all of the pain that you have endured, no matter how great or small, and use it for His glory (Rom 8:28) and for your good.

The work of taking an honest look into your life will require you to go back to your earliest memories and dig up the first feelings, emotions, thoughts, and expectations you had as a child. This is your first writing assignment. I will provide you with some questions as a guide to help you go back into the recesses of your heart and rediscover pain that may have been covered up long ago. The pain must be rooted out because it's the lock to the vault around your heart that affects your behavior today. Answering the questions will cause you to reach back into the beauty and mystery that God originally placed within you. Every heart is created by God in a specific way of being sustained and fulfilled only through a relationship with Him. Real transcendence, or self-worth, will only be felt and experienced when the beauty you seek and the mystery you crave come together in fulfillment through your relationship with Jesus Christ. Living as you were created to live, working with God in your passion, you will achieve your highest need level – transcendence. You will know what it was like when God walked with Adam and Eve in the cool of the day, as He walks with you each day covering you in His presence.

The questions will also help you identify where the pain specifically originated in your childhood. The possibility that the pain was encountered through interaction with your parents is very high. It is important to understand that this exercise is not intended to determine fault, but is a guide to map out and realize where the pain first entered your heart. Some people have a hard time being honest about the pain they encountered because the affection for their parents is so strong. Remember, the reason a parent hurts a child is not often deliberate, but comes from the unresolved pain they have also endured. Their pain manifests itself and they do the best they can, but often injured parents unknowingly injure their own children. As you encounter pain from a parent or any other significant person in your life, don't blame them by taking a victim's position, but practice the act of compassionate obedience and see them as someone who has also been hurt and needs love just like you do.

No one is asking you to discount the severity of the pain you encountered in your childhood. Discovering this pain may also uncover some hidden feelings toward the person or people from which the pain first arrived. One of THE most critical pieces of your freedom rests in your forgiveness of others. You must forgive those who have sinned against you and hurt you – regardless of what they did. Without forgiveness your freedom will be a futile pursuit. Jesus says in Mark 11:25, *"And whenever you stand praying, forgive, if you have anything against anyone, so that your Father also who is in heaven may forgive you your trespasses."* Forgiving others is a prerequisite to receiving forgiveness yourself. Remember this is not the forgiveness resulting in salvation, because God offered that forgiveness through the death of Jesus Christ. This is the forgiveness that brings freedom and releases you from the bondage that is applied to your heart through unforgiveness.

If there is a person in your life that is coming to your mind right now, please put this book down, and begin to pray and tell God how you truly feel. Proclaim that person's name and simply declare, to Jesus, that you forgive that person. Do it out loud. There may be more than one name, list them and declare forgiveness over those people. You are not excusing their actions by forgiving them. Don't let the enemy tell you that lie. You are actually setting your own heart free for Jesus by releasing yourself from the bondage of unforgiveness. Forgiveness is so critical; don't miss this opportunity to release yourself into Jesus care and protection. In some cases you may need to go to the person and mend the relationship. Whatever the Lord is asking you to do, do not delay – just obey.

The purpose of discovering the pain and the avenue through which it came is to allow you to take responsibility for your sinful reactions once the pain arrived. Our world is full of psychology that is designed to blame life circumstances and give excuses to people for their behavior. However, when we stand before Almighty God, none of us have an excuse for our behavior, regardless of the circumstances we have encountered. The sin you or I commit is our sin alone – Rom 3:23 tells us that all have sinned and fall short of the glory of God. The wages of that sin is death according to Romans 6:23, but the gift of God is eternal life. You are responsible for your sin. The reason you must look back to the place where pain entered your life is because you are responsible for the lies you started to believe as soon as you felt the pain. It's the lie in your heart that motivated the sinful reaction, and today is continuing to motivate your coping mechanisms.

Eve was responsible for the lie she believed, even though the cunning serpent was the one that brought the doubts to her ears. The lie she believed as we discussed earlier caused her to sin, that sin was Eve's responsibility alone. The lies you believe because of the pain you have received are the root cause for your addictive behavior, and the root cause of your coping mechanisms today. By going back and digging it up you will be obeying the Word through your confession and you will learn to reverse the lies by replacing them with the truth.

As the truth takes hold in your heart, you will find freedom from the grip that the pain has held for so long. The reason you still search for significance and security through your coping mechanisms is that you believe they are both missing in your life. You will continue to search for what you cannot have as long as you continue looking in the wrong place. The relationship of freedom that Jesus desires with you is the only source of significance and security. So as you answer the following questions take out a separate piece of paper and write a short paragraph for each answer identifying your feelings along the way. Be as complete and thorough as you can. You will use the answers to these questions later to write out your full autobiography which will be your second writing assignment. As you answer, think about how each answer relates to the ways that you thought you would feel more significant or more secure through your actions.

Significance and Security

1. *Children are born with dreams of becoming someone important, of doing something that will have a great impact on those they love, and to have something significant to bring them transcendence. What were your childhood dreams to:*

   a. *Be*

   b. *Do*

    c. Have

2. *Were those childhood dreams realized?   If not how were they stopped?*

    a. Who hurt you the most when you look back at your childhood?

    b. Were you ever told to get your head out of the clouds and stop all that dreaming?   Or were you told that you would never accomplish anything?   Or did the person who hurt you disagree with your idea of what was important?

    c. Were you ever punished for just being a child, as opposed to punishment that was justified by your misconduct?

3. *Did your father or mother praise you for your accomplishments, and how did their praise make you feel? Did you believe it was genuine or contrived?*

    a. Do you remember times when they didn't praise you but you wish they would have, and how did you respond to the way it made you feel?

    b. Were there times they praised you, even though you felt like you did not deserve the praise?   How did you respond to those feelings?

4. *Did your father or mother pay close attention to you and did they share in the things you enjoyed doing?*

    a. Did your father support you in the things you enjoyed, or only when you were involved in the things he enjoyed?   How did you respond to those feelings? Answer the same question regarding your mother's support.

5. *If your father was present in your life as you grew up – did he tell you that he loved you, did he show you affection through hugs or otherwise? How did you respond to the feelings it created?*

6. *Were you ever physically or sexually abused as a child, adolescent, or teen? Explain the circumstances and your response to what happened.*

7. *What are your earliest memories of how your family expressed their emotions?*

   a. *Were you allowed to express emotion? If so how did you express emotion as a child?*

   b. *How do you express your emotion today?*

8. *What are your earliest memories of your mother and father's communication with each other, and how did it make you feel?*

   a. *Did your father or mother communicate their wishes to you individually when you were growing up, did they set clear expectations and were they realistic with them? How did you respond to their treatment of you regarding your inability to please them? Or your inability to displease them?*

9. *Was your home a safe place to say what you thought?*

   a. *Did your family communicate openly about difficult subjects or problems that arose, and how did it make you feel?*

10. Were there subjects in your home that were considered taboo; issues such as sex, physical anatomy, drugs, pornography, etc.?

    a. If there were taboos – how did you learn about them, and how did you feel and respond to what you learned?

11. Were you granted tremendous freedom from your parents, or were you governed with strict rules of curfew, playmates, social restrictions, music restrictions, television restrictions, etc.?

    a. Which end of the spectrum of discipline did you find yourself – closer to "I could do no wrong", or closer to "I could do no right", and how did you respond to the feelings it created?

12. Who introduced you to Jesus Christ and how old were you when you met Him?

    a. What was your introduction to the ways of Jesus? A love relationship, or rules to follow and things not to do?

    b. What has been your response to the relationship you have with Jesus?

As you can see, these questions are intended to focus in on your childhood dreams revolving around the person you wanted to be, the things you wanted to do, and the things you wanted to have. Subconsciously the significance and security your heart desired were wrapped up in these things. As you discover the place where the pain entered your heart through the loss of these dreams you should also be able to see how you began to cope with the pain. Your answers should be written out with as much detail as possible.

Once you have finished answering these questions it is important that you share them with someone who you can trust. When it came time for me to share I went to my life group leader – even though he didn't know the process I was going through, he was gracious enough to listen and to keep it confidential. If you are married, I believe it is important that you share these things with your husband or wife eventually, but often it is best if you share these things for the first time with a person of the same sex. By sharing first with your friend, family member, pastor, or small group leader you will experience freedom from the shame that will allow you to eventually share with your spouse.

Your Team

Reading these answers out loud to a trusted person is the starting point of many things you will be confessing and sharing through this journey. It will make sense for you to explain to the person you share with that you are walking through this process because you love Jesus and desire His freedom. If you are single, again I would recommend sharing with a person of the same sex who you can confide in. I am praying that God will lead you to the right people. In some cases you will share with more than one person and these people will be your accountability team. God put His church together in fellowship for this very reason.

I can't emphasize enough the importance of verbalizing these things aloud to another person. James 5:16 tells us how healing comes through confessing one to another. Your verbal admission is faith with works, which is pleasing to the Lord. Pray and trust the Lord to grant you the courage it will take to express yourself openly with honest transparency. It won't be easy, and the enemy will try to convince you that you need to keep quiet. But don't listen to the lies any more, be strong and courageous – your freedom is worth it.

As you share with those in your team, you are also opening up the opportunity to disciple them through the same process in the future. The point of being willing to walk through the hard work of freedom is not so that you can arrive at an elite spiritual destination, but so that you can live out the great commission for Jesus Christ. He told us to go and make disciples of all nations, baptizing them in the name of the Father, and the Son, and the Holy Spirit, teaching them to obey all that Jesus commands, and not to have fear because He is with His disciples to the very end of the age (Matthew 28:19-20). My prayer is that once you have walked through your journey into freedom that you will take this book and will share it with the people in your life who are also struggling to encounter God's true love because of their own coping mechanisms and trapped hearts.

Remember, as you walk the staircase of compassionate obedience, falls will come, but confession and repentance will allow you to stand again and take the next step. Be honest and transparent as you journey – not only does it offer healing, but God will use it to challenge and grow those around you.

Discipleship

Some of the people who have come for counseling find themselves in a struggle as they begin this practical work and the need to confess. One of the reasons for their struggle is found in the lack of understanding about what it means to be a disciple of Jesus Christ. Jesus told us in John 8:31-32 *"So Jesus said to the*

Jews who had <u>believed him</u>, 'If you abide in my word, you are truly my disciples, and you will know the truth, and the truth will set you free. (underline mine)'" Jesus also told us in Luke 14:33 *"So therefore, any one of you who does not renounce all that he has cannot be my disciple."* Jesus prior to that verse also lays down some difficult words in Luke 14:26-27 *"If anyone comes to me and does not hate his own father and mother and wife and children and brothers and sisters, yes, and even his own life, he cannot be my disciple. Whoever does not bear his own cross and come after me cannot be my disciple."* These words and others that the Holy Spirit shared with us about discipleship are the reason that many walked away from Jesus in John 6:60-66.

As I stated previously, many people don't like the consequences that they feel as a result of a particular sin pattern in their life, but they also do not want to separate themselves from the temporary thrill that the sin pattern provides. It goes back to the original lie that Eve believed: "Jesus isn't enough, so therefore we also need other things." People who have found themselves in this situation become very discouraged because, even though they walk in compassionate obedience, and do the hard work to discover their past and confess, they are still not gaining the freedom found through intimacy with Jesus Christ. To help you avoid that kind of frustration, I hope to help you understand the cost of discipleship.

How would you feel if you desperately loved someone and desired their love with all of your heart, but instead of loving you, that person ignored you to go to the movies, to play some video games, to go to some concerts, watch some TV, or go to the bars and clubs, to spend hours on the internet seeing who messaged their Facebook account, or spent countless hours planning their next trip to relax without you? You would never be able to achieve intimacy with someone who gave themselves to the busy-ness of this life instead of spending time with you. You would be grieved if your love for someone was met with that kind of distraction. To love someone who doesn't want to give you the time of day would be heartbreaking. It is similar to what Jeremiah 3:20 says, *"But like a woman unfaithful to her husband, so you have been unfaithful to me, O house of Israel."* Two verses later God says, *"Return, faithless people; I will cure you of backsliding."* He wants pure intimacy. He says in the next breath, *"If you will return, O Israel, return to Me."* That verse is the voice of your Creator beckoning you to come into His presence.

Real discipleship costs us everything in this life – the word Oswald Chambers used is "abandon."[ix] The heart that is free is the heart that can be abandoned because it is willing to throw itself out upon God at any risk, believing in God's goodness. A trapped heart cannot live abandoned because protection is the ultimate goal. John 14:21 says of Jesus' true disciples, *"Whoever has my commandments and keeps them, he it is who loves me. And he who loves me will be loved by my Father, and I will love him and manifest myself to him."* Jesus makes it very clear that discipleship costs you the right to your own life. The relationship of freedom in Jesus Christ is predicated by the willingness to part with or to add to your life anything and everything as He commands.

Jesus didn't bring religion into this world, He brought relationship. When we begin to tell other people what things they have to give up, unless stated in Scripture, we immediately become religious and separate from the heart of Jesus. We cannot judge one another, but one thing is true of the disciple whose heart is set free – he is willing to part with or join with anything God commands. This is impossible for the natural man. That is why Jesus is our Savior – He didn't just teach us and leave us, He imparted His Spirit to us and the step of faith by a believer into the impossible is met with the manifestation of Jesus' power to walk in it. There is nothing more powerful, fun, beautiful, or adventurous on this earth than living out the life of Jesus by the power of the Holy Spirit in our mortal flesh. Discipleship isn't giving up anything really – it's actually gaining everything!

The disciple of Jesus Christ experiences the relationship of oneness and intimacy by the supernatural work of the Holy Spirit who transforms the natural man into the divine nature of Jesus Christ. Freedom doesn't come because God takes something away from you – it comes because God changes the source of your nature. Your life exhibits fruit that is only possible for the Son of God to fulfill because the Spirit has manifested Jesus' power in your mortal body (2 Cor 4:10-11). Jesus said He is the Way, the Truth, and the Life. John 8 says we will know the Truth and the Truth will set us free – it is Jesus manifested in your life and only by Him that you will experience your Genesis Moment and the release from captivity and burdens you are longing for. True contentment is found as Jesus' disciple.

Freedom will continue to elude the person who doesn't want to give it all over to the Lord. In reality, Jesus may be your Savior by faith, but He may not be your Lord because you are withholding ownership of your entire life. Jesus words in John 8:31-38 were spoken to the Jews who "believed him." Jesus' first response is to clarify who will truly be a disciple; He said it is the one who abides in His Word. They are confused by His clarification because they think they are already free. He goes on to condemn their thinking because they do not belong to Him. Only a son remains in the house forever, He says. Jesus' Word in

John 8:36 says, "if" the Son sets you free you will be free indeed. Only when He decides will your freedom be possible. Verse 37 tells us that His word cannot abide in them, *"because my word finds no place in you."* Verse 38 tells us why – *"you do what you have heard from your father."* The small "f" father is the devil – John 8:44 speaks of the devil and his language of lies.

The reason you have not entered into freedom is because you still believe the devil's lies. None of us are born as children of God; only Jesus Christ was born as God's Son. He is the only begotten son (John 3:16); therefore, all the rest of mankind are born as children of the devil. That means you and me – we were born speaking our father's language of lies. Those lies took root in our hearts as young children, and though you have been saved by faith and God's grace, you have not found freedom because the truth has no place in your heart due to the lies that still hold residence. This is why we must identify the lies and allow God's Word to break their strongholds. When God's Word has the place to abide in your heart, you will no longer be a slave to sin, but you will be set free because Jesus is the Word (John 1:1), and He is the Truth (John 14:6), and He will manifest His power through your heart (John 14:21). Jesus never had any addictions, therefore when He transforms your life by making Himself your source, neither will you continue in your sin (1 John 3:9).

Only when we fully surrender and renounce all that we have, will we come to experience Jesus as Lord. Do it today – don't wait and struggle through your burdens and captivity indefinitely. Humble yourself and admit that you are being controlled by what you have heard from the devil (John 8:38) before you entered the kingdom by faith. Believe only in Jesus – He will set you free.

Coping Mechanisms

Jesus goes on in John 8 to speak about the confirmation of being a disciple. The confirmation is found in John 8:42 *"Jesus said to them, 'If God were your Father, you would love me, for I came from God and I am here. I came not of my own accord, but he sent me.'"* The evidence of freedom in our lives is when the love relationship with Jesus is established, and not when you come to an intellectual understanding of the Bible. The problem I was encountering in my own life was an inability to truly love Jesus because the lies I believed were preventing me from giving or receiving love at all. The diagram below shows this trap by the circle around the heart – the behaviors in your life today that you want to be free from are your coping mechanisms born out of self-protection, not born out of love.

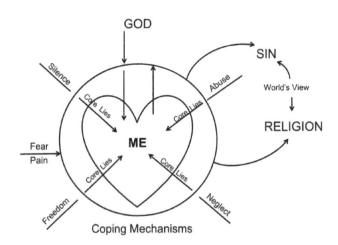

Coping Mechanisms

As you look back at the answers to the questions you wrote out, hopefully you were able to identify the specific pain that you encountered as a child. I have given a few examples of pain in the diagram. The pain is often felt as a result of the response from the person upon whom a child has placed the highest value. A common significant pain in children comes from the father in the form of silence: silence, if the father is in the home or silence because the father has abandoned the home. Children look for approval for their accomplishments, if they are met with silence it is received as "not good enough to get a response". The core lie settles in the child's heart that they are not good enough. That child will then be convinced to try harder and to do everything perfect in order to gain approval. This core lie eventually causes children to recognize silence as a time to become the center of attention. From the core lie, the child begins to believe this thought "My efforts are never good enough, so there must be something wrong with me." This is translated as pain and in order to protect against that negative feeling a coping mechanism is developed in order to prove to himself and the world that he **is** good enough.

To help explain let's go back to the example I used earlier of the young man who said he wanted freedom from his addiction to pornography. When he first learned of the opportunity to walk through this process he was very excited. Due to his struggle, he would drop off his computer at my house so that he was not tempted at home. He would only pick up the computer when he needed it for school, but even in those short periods of time he would fall to his coping mechanism of watching pornography. So together we dug into his past and his pain. He went through the first process of answering the questions in this chapter.

We unearthed the key pain in his life. He realized that at a young age he viewed his father as the person of highest value in his life. He saw his father's job, his father and mother's relationship, and his father's relationship with the children as the ultimate goal to be reached. This young man believed that his father must have achieved the greatest significance and security through these things and therefore he wanted to be just like him. But at a very critical developmental stage in this young man's life, his father made a seemingly innocent comment about his son's physical size and referred to him as "little."

The young man even today is still smaller than most people his age and that pain still has a hold on his life. The lie that he began to believe was that only the bigger guys would get the good job, the wife, and the children. Facing his fear of not measuring up this young man began to cope with his inadequacy privately through fantasy which ultimately led him to pornography. Pornography continued to allow him to live with the lie and believe that he was finding the significance and security he longed for, but in reality he was settling for a cheap and sinful counterfeit – and the shame and emptiness it brought was proof that it wasn't the answer.

The truth this young man lacked is found in God's Word which says we are formed and knit together in our mother's wombs. Before one of our days is lived, God has seen them all. (Psalm 139) God does not make mistakes in His creation and a relationship with God is not contingent on anything but Jesus' sacrifice. We all can be made perfect in Jesus and no one needs any counterfeit to provide counterfeit significance. The truth will set men free.

I wish there was a great ending to that story, but when this young man had discovered his pain and coping mechanism he stopped seeking out the Lord's truth. I don't know to this day how he is doing, but I do know that Jesus wants him to experience true love, just like he wants you to experience true love. Pain comes in many forms – others have had parents that never gave them any rules. This formed the belief in their hearts that there was no limit to exceed for punishment or for excellence – therefore it eventually created the coping mechanism of pushing the limits and living to the extreme. The pain of abuse has convinced children that they are dirty and worthless and the coping mechanism often a result is seeking out repeated unhealthy relationships. This often results in the recreation of the same circumstances that brought them the original pain. The list can go on and on, but right now you need to seek the Lord by discovering the reality of the pain that you once experienced and ask God to truly reveal how it led to the coping mechanisms that you are dealing with today.

Identify

Once you have discovered the pain, it is important to identify by name each of your coping mechanisms. You will be able to identify the coping mechanisms by correlating the feelings of insignificance and insecurity to the ways you tried to make yourself feel better. You began to deal with those feelings of inadequacy by whatever means possible, and to this day if you struggle with addiction you are continuing to try and find significance and security because you were created to experience transcendence. Identifying your coping mechanisms is necessary because they are the symptoms that will lead you back to your core lies. God wants to give you truth in place of your core lies. The type of coping mechanism you have developed and perfected is related to the type of insignificance or insecurity you originally felt and the feelings that you still recognize. Looking at the truth about the insignificance or insecurity you felt and denying the lie by replacing it with God's Truth and acting upon it will bring you into your Genesis Moment.

From our example of the young man earlier, he identified his idea of greatest significance as that which would come through a life just like his father's. He wanted to "BE" just like his father. He also believed that his dad's significance came from his physical size and his job – so what the young man wanted to "DO" was to get bigger and become smarter. But with significance every child also needs security in the form of love and so the young man wanted to "HAVE" a loving relationship with a beautiful wife and children. The young man believed that significance and security were sourced in what he wanted to BE, DO, and HAVE. Learning that he was small, and then struggling with some learning challenges in school – he began to believe lies about himself instead of the way God truly saw him. His reactions eventually formed coping mechanisms and ultimately led him to an addiction to pornography, which was his strongest coping mechanism.

Begin to make a list of the coping mechanisms you turn to when you feel the fear of pain coming on. If you are an addict that would be the top of the list, but even addicts can't turn to their addiction all the time and so a second level coping mechanism that is publicly acceptable is often an alternative. For instance, in my life when I couldn't act out in my coping mechanism of sexual addiction, I would turn to food for temporary satisfaction. Behavior like that is often called emotional eating, but truly it was my way of satiating my flesh so I didn't feel the possible emptiness that pain had once brought. It was a second best coping mechanism when my primary one could not be accessed.

Once your list is complete, it is important that you read the list to someone on your accountability team. Let them know the areas where your strongholds exist and ask them to pray with you for God's power to destroy these strongholds. The key is that you must believe.

Believe

There is no stronger force in the human world than belief. Belief is the seed from which the root of faith grows and when faith sprouts fruit is produced. This is true 100% of the time for 100% of people. The only difference between the person who follows Jesus Christ and the person who doesn't is their direction of belief. All people produce fruit, but only people who believe in Jesus Christ and obey what He said will produce fruit in keeping with repentance (Matthew 3:8). All others will produce the fruit of dead works (Romans 6:21). But in both cases the fruit can be traced back to the seed of their belief.

As you continue to seek the Lord in this journey toward being set free from your coping mechanisms, you need to settle the belief issue in your heart. You need to stand firm on the promises of God's Word and believe that He is able to set you free by removing these besetting sins and burdens from your life. He who is faithful will do it (1 Thess 5:24). Without faith it is impossible to please God (Heb 11:6) and so you must believe in His power over your life.

In the next chapter we will carry forward what you have discovered about your pain and coping mechanisms as you begin to shape your autobiography. As these pains created core lies, these lies motivated some actions in your life for which you are now most likely extremely embarrassed and ashamed of. For some the pain was so intense that some memories were actually completely blotted out. In these cases you will need to pray and ask God to reveal to you everything you need to know to deal with your past. He will do it as you remain honest and transparent. He will be faithful to bring to mind all that must be dealt with. The next chapter will have more instruction on writing out your autobiography and you will have yet another opportunity to sit with your accountability team to express your love for God through your obedience to His Word.

Reflections:

1. Is there anyone that you have not forgiven? If there is take the time now to speak their name to the Lord and tell Him that you forgive them out loud.

2. As you answer the questions on pages 54 & 55 keep the ideas of significance and security at the forefront. As you write your answers think about how you were told that you were unimportant and that you were unlovable.

3. List your top 3 biggest fears about looking back into your past? Write them out and surrender them to the Lord asking Him to give you courage to overcome those fears.

Chapter 5

The Story of Your Soul

Before writing your autobiography, it is important for you to realize the value of each human soul. You may be combating feelings of defeat or lies that the enemy is speaking over you. You may be hearing things like "you aren't important enough to God to be set free," or that "your situation is worse than all others and wouldn't warrant God's power." Those are lies, and it's your responsibility to expel those lies with the Truth.

One of the byproducts of addiction and trapped hearts is the myriad of lies that we have convinced ourselves are true. Addictions leave the addict with a distorted sense of reality and often times that reality creates a devaluation of life. For some addicts the only way out of their turmoil is suicide because their lives have been so devalued through the destructive nature of their sin. That kind of destruction is what Satan strives for in everyone's life.

God's Word tells us that we are living in a fallen world, a world where the intentions of God for His creation were cursed by sin as Adam and Eve chose to act outside of God's will. In the very moment that Eve, and then Adam, stepped outside the boundary of God's perfect plan, sin entered the world, and mankind was forever stricken with a curse. The verses in Genesis 3:17-20 recount the curse of man when God says to Adam, *"Cursed is the ground because of you; through painful toil you will eat of it all the days of your life. It will produce thorns and thistles for you, and you will eat the plants of the field. By the sweat of your brow you will eat your food until you return to the ground, since from it you were taken; for dust you are, and to dust you will return."*

Our wrong view of self is a product of this curse and directly attributed to the sin that entered the world. God's intentions for the world are found in the first two chapters of the Bible in which God calls all that He has created 'good.' He made a perfect world to be inhabited by perfect people, who by choice were able to love Him and have perfect communion with Him. He even went so far as to create man in His image so that they could experience the physical glory of His image. Even to be a shadow of the living God is a privilege to which words cannot be ascribed.

Beauty

To start, I want to use the colors of God's Word to paint for you the picture of how important you are to the Creator of the Universe. As God created the world, each day He proclaimed it to be good, and once the earth was formed and the sun and moon and stars, birds, fish, and animals were all made, He created man. Here is the point – God knew that in no way could man ever meet his own needs – God knew that at every minute of every day man would be reliant on Him for existence. Without God meeting the needs of mankind we all would cease to exist.

In spite of having to meet the needs of all people continuously, even the ones He knew would ultimately reject Him; He still chose to create them so that He could have intimacy with those who choose to love Him. Does that register with you? Read it over again. A sovereign, perfect Creator created a being that would require a never ending supply of oxygen, sunlight, food, water, shelter, and protection – a completely needy human so that not only could He enjoy our company, but we could also experience His presence in an intimate relationship. Oscar Thompson in his book *Concentric Circles* defines love as "meeting needs".[x] God loves you constantly because with every breath you breathe He is meeting your needs.

The God of the universe, the Divine authority, the Beginning and the End did it all because His nature is love and He loves you and me, His love endures forever – it will never cease. He specifically dreamed of you before the beginning of time and knew exactly what you would look like. He knew exactly how you would act, what kind of personality you would have, and what you would choose to do with your life. In spite of knowing about all the rebellious choices you would make, He still created you because of His great love. God's greatest desire is for His created people to love Him and choose to follow Him so that we will be intimately connected to Him for all of eternity. Isaiah 43:6-7 says, *"I will say to the north, 'Give them up!' and to the south, 'Do not hold them back,' Bring my sons from afar and my daughters from the ends of the earth – everyone who is called by my name, whom I created for my glory, whom I formed and made."* Isaiah 45:18 says, *"For this is what the Lord says – He who created the heavens, he is God; He who fashioned and made the earth, He founded it; He did not create it to be empty, but formed it to be inhabited."* You must see that it is not an accident that you exist and that you are here on this earth reading this book right now.

Recently I had a man approach me with a question after a Bible study. He said to me "I have a little girl and she is everything to me, there is nothing that she can do to ever make me not love her or want to be with her. Even if she stabbed me or hurt me, I would still love her and be her daddy. There is absolutely nothing that would make me not love her. But when you talk about God, you say I will go to hell and forever be separated from Him if I don't obey Him. How can you say He wants to be my father, when I would never do that to my daughter, but He would do that to me?"

His question is a valid one, but his question also points out the very nature of God. He is the Father, the one who loves His children perfectly. God desperately loves you as His child. The difference is found in the fact that God is perfect and righteous and just. There is nothing unclean or impure about God and that is what separates Him from the very ones He created. When Adam and Eve sinned, they broke the connection with God, God did not reject them for their imperfection; they rejected God by choosing imperfection.

I asked my friend how it would make him feel if his daughter, whom he loves so desperately, was to turn her back on him, and tell him that she will not obey anything he says, if she would tell him that she is not his daughter, and that she doesn't love him – if she would tell him, she only loves herself and is leaving to go her own way. My friend said "Wow – that would devastate me." I responded, "That's exactly how God feels when you reject Him, you are rejecting His love." When my friend related the pain of losing his daughter's love with God's love for him he came under heavy conviction and decided to surrender his life to Jesus. It was the Holy Spirit calling my friend.

My friend was able to have a relationship with his daughter because like all humans, they are both sinners. Two sinners are capable of having a relationship because there is nothing that separates them spiritually. However, God is perfect, and therefore cannot be united to anything less than perfect. He cannot accept an imperfect person into a relationship with Himself unless there is way to make the imperfect, perfect.

Perfect Humility

Each year we celebrate Christmas and even now I am typing this on Christmas Day while this idea is fresh in my mind. We have already spoken of creation, how God so humbly created everything for man. Sin brought the curse to what He had created. He then humbly gave us the Law through Moses as He dwelled above the Ark of the Covenant, despite mankind's imperfection. However, His people still chose to reject Him and His presence.

After 400 years of silence, Jesus humbly entered the world from heaven – in the form of humanity – though righteously divine. In His humility He remained righteous through all of His choices on the earth, being perfect at the time of His death. Yet while He was alive and perfect, man rejected Him to the point of death, where He gave Himself over to die. Jesus humbly went to the cross – as Philippians 2:8 records, *"And being found in appearance as a man, he humbled himself and became obedient to death – even death on a cross!"*

Through this death, He made a way for man's imperfection to be justified through faith in what Jesus Christ had done in loving obedience to God the Father. In His humility he then ascended to heaven, because as John 16:7 says *"But I tell you the truth: It is for your good that I am going away. Unless I go away, the Counselor will not come to you; but if I go, I will send him to you."* And even now He sits humbly on the throne in Heaven as Revelation 5:6 says, *"Then I saw a Lamb, looking as if it had been slain, standing in the center of the throne, encircled by the four living creatures and the elders."* This humility is shown by His ability to receive all *power, wealth, wisdom, strength, honor and glory, and praise,* without being proud. In this way, our Lord allows all of His creation to worship Him, as was His intention, which is how we display our love for Him. Without a humble recipient of our worship, we would not have a way to experience intimacy at all, especially with our Creator, which is why we exist in the first place. What a Glorious God we serve!

The Task

With this view of God's value of your soul, you can begin to put together the autobiography of your life. Start with your earliest memories and begin to tell the story of you. The earliest memories you can recall today might not be the earliest, but it is the best place to start. So many people have used coping mechanisms to wipe out memories that were extremely traumatic. Do not be frightened by these memories when they come back. In fact, ask God to bring back any memories that have been suppressed so that you can deal with them and experience the Lord's healing of the pain. Do not be surprised that these memories will come back after you have started to write. If they do, be faithful to include them.

Your autobiography should include the situations you encountered early in life that inflicted the greatest pain in your heart. Remember, trying to escape the pain is what created your coping mechanisms. So many times people begin to write their autobiography from a perspective of their own innocence, after all you were only a child and this pain was undeserved. That is true. However, continue to remember that although the pain was not your fault, how you responded to the pain is your fault.

The autobiography will give you opportunity to describe where the pain came from, but more importantly it needs to be written as a confession of the sinful ways that you dealt with it. The goal is to confess your sinful actions from your childhood until the present – especially as they relate to your coping mechanisms. You will not be able to recount each and every individual experience, but you will be able to put together the specific experiences that shaped your life.

Job 36:8-12 says, *"And if they are bound in chains and caught in the cords of affliction, then he declares to them their work and their transgressions, that they are behaving arrogantly. He opens their ears to instruction and commands that they return from iniquity. If they listen and serve him, they complete their days in prosperity, and their years in pleasantness. But if they do not listen, they perish by the sword and die without knowledge."* In the passage, Elihu is extolling God for His greatness as he talks with Job, but he is also giving us a tremendous key to freedom. God declares to us our iniquity, and we know that confession brings healing, yet when people refuse to confess their sin and repent, they are in fact sinning arrogantly. Your autobiography is another exercise in humility.

By now I am sure that you have identified your coping mechanisms. I also trust that you are able to map those coping mechanisms back to the circumstances in your childhood, adolescence, and maybe young adulthood. As you do – describe the actions you were committing and also the motives behind your actions. Often we are faithful to confess our actions, but we fail to repent of our motives. The motive is often more difficult to deal with because it carries more weight. Do not let the enemy intimidate you into avoiding this important step. The Lord is the One who judges the thoughts and intentions of the heart. We must confess not just the actions, but the motives behind those actions. Allow this autobiography to bring all the darkness to the light – as the Word said in Job; you will complete your days in prosperity, and your years in pleasantness if you will listen and serve God.

The form of your autobiography should be that of a story or an essay. When I had written mine it ended up being about 7 pages single-space type printed. There were a number of critical and hidden things that needed to come to the surface. Depending on how long you have been dealing with your coping mechanisms you may find yours is much longer, or maybe far shorter. There is no "right" length – just be thorough to cover all the hidden areas of your life, especially things you thought you would never tell anyone. Once you have written it out and you believe there is nothing else that could come back to memory it is time to read it to someone on your team.

Confession

Of all the steps of this practical exercise, I will say I believe this may be the toughest step for most people to actually complete. I have witnessed in a number of cases that people are willing to discover their pain, write up their answers to the questions of security and significance, identify their coping mechanisms, and write out their autobiography. But these same people seem to stop when it comes to actually scheduling a time to sit down with someone and read it aloud. I want to exhort you, as difficult as it may seem this is one of your most critical steps toward freedom. Satan will lie and tell you it isn't necessary, but James 5:16 says, *"Therefore, confess your sins to one another and pray for one another, that you may be healed. The prayer of a righteous person has great power as it is working."* Believe and act on the Truth and you will receive healing as you are faithful to obey God's Word.

Again, if you are married, I suggest reading your autobiography first to your trusted friend of the same sex. Often you will be covering areas of sexuality and sexual sin that have been hidden for a long time. The pressure and shock of sharing this for the first time with your spouse may be too much to allow you to follow through. By sharing first with your friend you will find God's healing to be sufficient to remove the perceived pressure you thought would exist and will allow you to open your heart to your spouse. When two people become one flesh the sins brought into the marriage can also have far reaching consequences in both people. Bringing this autobiography into the light will allow God's healing in your relationship as well. It may also spur your spouse on to walk through this same process and give you the opportunity to support and encourage.

I have often described to people the sensation that comes from telling the truth through reading their autobiography as BB's hitting a tile floor. Many times people live in shame for such a long time because they fear what people will say of them if they told the truth about their lives. This fear of other's reactions is what keeps people in bondage to their coping mechanisms. But time and time again as I sit with someone reading their autobiography this huge sense of relief comes over them. The hidden part of life seems like bombs that will shock people and bring total shame, yet when the person is faithful to confess, those bombs turn into BB's and when they hit the floor they bounce and roll away. This is how God brings the healing through our confession. So do not be afraid to share. Even before you write it out ask your accountability team to make sure that you follow through and read it to them.

In more than one case the person who was reading their autobiography had committed some sins they considered "extreme." These people experienced fear in sharing some issues that they believed they would carry with them to the grave. Some of these "extreme" sinful situations included sexually abusing a younger family member, homosexuality, adultery, rape, etc. However, regardless of how shame-filled these people felt, every one of them experienced the same relief as they confessed these things aloud. Do not let your "extreme" sin prevent you from the life and love God has in store for you. Write your autobiography and read it aloud to your team.

You might wonder why you can't just burn it after you write it down. As I mentioned before, I believe the reason that God's Word says we are to confess to one another is because once I have told someone the truth about my life, I can never back up and deny it. There is a reality of commitment when you confess it to another person. Truthfully, God already knows all the sin and every instance of coping mechanism you have committed. He is not interested in you telling Him something He already knows, but He is interested in you owning something He knows and agreeing with Him about it. Once you own the sin, in other words confess it, He is faithful and just to forgive you your sins and cleanse you of all unrighteousness (1 John 1:9).

Once you have read your autobiography to your team, it may be worth keeping a copy. I still have my original copy and I have read it many times to many people who have walked through this process of freedom. By being willing to be vulnerable to someone else, you can build up their confidence in being vulnerable enough to read their own autobiography. That may not be what God wants you to do, but I do know God wants you to be set free so that you can help set others free. He uses our pain to comfort others. 2 Corinthians 1:3-4 says, *"Blessed be the God and Father of our Lord Jesus Christ, the Father of mercies and God of all comfort, who comforts us in all our affliction, so that we may be able to comfort those who are in any affliction, with the comfort with which we ourselves are comforted by God."*

Life in Christ

I know this has been covered in early chapters, but the gospel is the key to freedom and it bears repeating. For too many, the idea of salvation has been regretfully diminished by self-seeking disobedient grace seekers. Many people teach a salvation that is grievously short of the true message put forth in the Bible. Many churches have lost the power of the Holy Spirit because they fail to preach the full gospel for which Jesus Christ lived and died. Your ability to overcome your addictions and sinful behaviors rests in the power of the Holy Spirit – a relationship through faith. There is only one way to live in a love relationship with God – to obey God's commands and thus receive eternal life supernaturally from the hand of God. You are then transferred into a new life, an inherited life that was predestined for you and for which God created you according to Psalm 33.

The gospel begins by getting the right perspective of yourself before a holy God, though you are a person desperately loved by God, you are a sinner and therefore separated from Him. Admitting your sin before God is the starting point of salvation. Forgiveness of sin occurred at the cross of Jesus Christ, when 2 Corinthians 5:21, *"God made him who had no sin to be sin for us, so that in him we might become the righteousness of God."* It is not that you must ask for forgiveness as a future event, but that you must accept, or receive the forgiveness already supplied by the cross. In Acts 26:18 Jesus says, *"to open their eyes and turn them from darkness to light, and from the power of Satan to God, so that they may receive forgiveness of sins and a place among those who are sanctified by faith in me."* The words *receive,* and *sanctified* are both referencing past action. You must receive what has already been given, and you must take your place.

What is Jesus referring to in these words in Acts? Ephesians 2:4-6 tells us what happened at the ascension of Christ, *"But because of His great love for us, God, who is rich in mercy, made us alive with Christ even when we were dead in transgressions – it is by grace you have been saved. And God raised us up with Christ and seated us with him in the heavenly realms in Christ Jesus."* This is the sanctified position that Jesus is referring to. Those who are going to inherit and accept the gift of grace have already been placed in the throne room of God at the time of Jesus' resurrection. The acceptance of this gift of God is not a future happening but rather a position for the believer to take. Neil Anderson says, "The moment you receive Christ, you take possession of what God did for you 2000 years ago".[xi] What does it then mean to receive Christ?

According to Romans 1, 2, and 3 it is clear that this receiving is only possible through faith. Romans 3:23 says, *"For all have sinned and fall short of the glory of God."* The first acknowledgement in a person's life to receive Christ is to admit that you are a sinner. As the example of my friend, he understood that he could not have a relationship with God because of his sin. This acknowledgement of sin is not a blanket statement that lumps all of your actions together, but rather, an acknowledgement of understanding that everything you have ever done on your own, apart from God, is sin.

As we read in Job 36, God commands that we confess the sin of our lives and humbly acknowledge that nothing is righteous in us, nothing! Upon acknowledging that this is true, we then must acknowledge Jesus. Romans 3:21 says, *"But now a righteousness from God, apart from the law, has been made known, to which the Law and the Prophets testify. This righteousness from God comes through faith in Jesus Christ to all who believe."* Verse 25 says, *"God presented him as a sacrifice of atonement, through faith in his blood."*

The Law, as stated in Romans 3:10-18 says that there is no way for a man to get to God through his own actions. The Law itself condemns all men because of sin which came through Adam. So just as the sin came into the world through Adam, grace came into the world through one man, Jesus Christ. For you to accept this you must accept in your heart that Jesus was placed into Mary's womb by the Holy Spirit from heaven, and was therefore not born of human seed. Jesus' life on this earth was righteous because He came from God. From the time of His birth to the time of His death, He was to remain righteous before God. The only way for Jesus to remain righteous was to follow all that God had given in the Law. Therefore Jesus, through every thought, word, and deed, remained sinless while on this earth – fulfilling the Law.

In this way, He was an acceptable offering for the sin of the world as we read in 2 Corinthians 5:21. That sin offering to God was then given by Jesus in the form of His life on the Cross where God was able to lay all the sin of the world onto Him and through the death of a perfectly innocent offering, God's righteous judgment was executed and His wrath satisfied. God in His love and mercy then raised Jesus from the dead defeating death and

103

Satan in one fell swoop, forever making a way for all men to come into His presence through faith in Jesus Christ.

A Holy God could not have had a relationship with any man had Jesus not paid the full penalty for the curse of sin upon the earth and with it the consequence of death. Because Jesus remained perfectly obedient to God all the days of His life, He was acceptable and became the righteousness that is spoken of in Romans 3. When you humbly acknowledge that everything you have done in your life apart from God is sin, and secondly that Jesus Christ was a real man who paid a real price for sin, you will then repent of your sin and turn from your way of life and by faith believe that the only way to live is through obedience to Jesus Christ.

Many people have been disillusioned by a false gospel that contains only knowledge. The true gospel is knowledge believed that produces action, which is faith. Your repentance means that you are no longer willing to walk in a way opposite of God and that you are 100% humbly willing to obey all that God commands.

This is not to be confused with perfection. Although someone may be 100% humbly willing, it does not mean that same person will be 100% accurate in hitting the mark each time. Each person will fall to things that cause sin just as Luke 17:1 says, *"Jesus said to His disciples: 'Things that cause people to sin are bound to come, but woe to that person through whom they come.'"* Jesus is explaining that we all will sin. Though we sin, grace is our supernatural covering that does not let us lose our position with God.

However, to remain clean before God, He has commanded confession as we have already covered. We must be humbly willing to obey every command that God puts forth in His word in order to say that we have truly repented. Acts 26:20 says, *"First*

104

to those in Damascus, then to those in Jerusalem and in all Judea, and to the Gentiles also, I preached that they should repent and turn to God and prove their repentance by their deeds." By that last statement it is clear that repentance does not exist in your life if you still desire to follow the ways of the world. Repentance is a turning away from. Confession is calling sin exactly what God calls it – sin. Those two things according to James help identify the person who has truly been regenerated through salvation. James 2:17 says, *"In the same way, faith by itself, if it is not accompanied by action, is dead."*

The only way to be saved is through God's creative work of speaking light into your heart and granting you faith. If you have not put your faith in Jesus Christ so that your life is marked by the evidence of repentance do it right now. Only God knows your heart, but that is exactly the point, ONLY He knows your heart and the second after you die there will only be one thing that matters – God's view of your life.

I heard a story told of a man who had pastored a church for a number of years who continued to struggle in his walk with the Lord. He went to another pastor and told him the struggles he was having. The other pastor told him that he didn't think he had ever been saved, to which the man replied to the effect of, "I'm so relieved you said that, I have wondered that for years." That day the man received his salvation and was changed. He humbly went back to his church to resign because of the hypocrisy, but one wise elder spoke up and said something to effect of, "Since we've had a pagan preacher this long, it would be best if you kept the job so we could have one that's born again."

You can go around the world proclaiming and preaching how others should see Jesus, or how others should know Jesus, and you can tell them to study the Bible all you want. But at the end of all their works and the end of their life, according to Matthew 7:21, there is only one thing that matters – God's view of their life. Matthew 7:21 says, *"Not everyone who says to me, 'Lord, Lord,' will enter the kingdom of heaven, but only he who does the will of my Father who is in heaven."* Verse 22 continues, *"Many will say to me on that day, 'Lord, Lord, did we not prophesy in your name, and in your name drive out demons and perform many miracles?' Then I will tell them plainly, 'I never knew you. Away from me, you evildoers!'"* It doesn't matter how many degrees from Seminary you might have, or who your greatest teacher was, or what you think the Bible says, or about how you think church should be run – the only thing that matters is how Jesus views your life.

Your freedom rests upon the starting point of a relationship – a genuine relationship with Jesus Christ. That relationship is also why your autobiography holds such a key to your progress toward freedom. A relationship built on lies is no relationship at all. Jesus has already made each saint free through His work on the cross. When we believe lies and act out of those lies we are failing to receive and live in the position Christ has already procured for us. Commit to Jesus and allow Him to bring you fully into the relationship He has with His Father. No one ever lived a freer life than the Lord Jesus Christ.

Alternative

The other alternative is that you are not saved and that you would rather choose the "fun" of sin over a relationship with Jesus Christ. You may act like a Christian and sound like Christian, but you may not be truly saved. Unfortunately the Word says there will be many like this. Jesus says in Matthew 7:13, *"Enter through the narrow gate. For wide is the gate and broad is the road that leads to destruction, and many enter through it. But small is the gate and narrow is the road that leads to life, and only a few find it."*

The question you need to answer is, "Are you going to be one of the few that find it?" Will you be the one who has finally had enough of your habitual sin patterns, secret sin, pain, burdens, and addiction that you are willing to call it sin before God and man, repent, and believe that Jesus can set you free? Solidify that decision in your heart – not your mind. Romans 10:10 says, *"For it is with your heart that you believe and are justified, and it is with your mouth that you confess and are saved."* Your mind cannot save you. Only a humble heart, a willing heart, a repentant heart will be saved!

You are so valuable to God! His desire to set you free is greater than your desire to be free. Allow the truth of God's Word to grant you the prosperous life of contentment we read about in Job 36. The real purpose of your life is not found in simply being saved, but is found by living in abundant love with Jesus Christ and fulfilling His purpose for your life.

A problem exists when Satan has infiltrated churches and hearts and started to create a false gospel that is keeping people from knowing the Truth. Every lie that man believes traps him further away from God.

Following God's Word will not only grant your heart the freedom to experience prosperity and contentment, but will also build true love in your heart for the Lord, your spouse, your children, your friends, and the people around you. Your heart will no longer be trapped by coping mechanisms but will roam free in God's creative hand to bring a dying world to salvation in Jesus Christ. God has great things in store for you.

Reflections:

1. Write your autobiography – get started.
   a. Start at your earliest memories of the pain from which the coping mechanisms came.
   b. Remember this is a confession, not indictment against those who hurt you, so identify them but focus on how you acted sinfully in your responses to the pain.
   c. Bring to light each of the areas of pain, each of the ways you dealt with it, and explain how the coping mechanisms in your life were perfected.
   d. You won't be able to identify all the sins you've ever committed, but identify and confess the motives behind acting out in your coping mechanisms.
   e. Be as honest and transparent as you can, do not hold anything back, and trust the Lord to help you remember and write.
   f. This is the story of your life and how you tried to live it apart from Jesus so let it all out.

2. Once it is written, do not delay – sit with your trusted friend and share what you have put on paper. Contentment is found in confession.

Chapter 6

A Heart of Steel

If you had to describe the heart that is beating within your chest right now I have to believe that you would be pretty accurate. We don't have to be doctors to understand what our hearts do within our bodies and how they function. We know it is a muscle controlled by an involuntary response from our nervous system to beat regularly, pumping life giving blood to all portions of our body. There are valves and ventricles and veins and arteries that run throughout the heart. The contraction of the muscle with faithful frequency keeps us alive. A heart attack is simply a heart that ceases to beat, no more contractions, just a motionless frozen muscle. If not revived by an outside force, an inactive heart equals death and the end of a life.

The spiritual heart of a man is also just as critical to life and freedom. There are only three ways the enemy attacks us – by making us want to be somebody, do something, or have something (the pride of life, the desires of the eyes, and the desires of the flesh - 1 John 2:16). Those are his tactics and they don't change.

Remember the Bible describes him as cunning and seeking those he may devour like a roaring lion. A lion goes for the weak, the slow, and the uneducated that cannot fight back. He makes an easy meal out of such prey. So as the enemy sees little children who do not yet have the Truth of God in their hearts, he begins a series of spiritual heart attacks, which we examined in the second chapter. If anyone has a series of heart attacks physically they will die, which is precisely the enemy's spiritual goal for every child. The enemy attacks our children's hearts, which is the very place that God designed for Himself. The enemy's success equates to millions of souls experiencing an eternal separation from God.

As you are experiencing a new level of awareness in your heart right now, you will also need to be on guard against these kinds of attacks. I pray that your heart is starting to break at the thought of what is going on around you. The freedom God wants you to experience is always for others, and especially for your children. The way you experienced pain was through your childhood, and now it becomes your responsibility to prevent that pain in the lives of the next generation. Allow your heart to break for the things that break God's heart. Remaining broken is part of the ongoing relationship we have with God. God said in Isaiah 66:2 *"'Has not my hand made all these things, and so they came into being?' declares the LORD. 'This is the one I esteem: he who is humble and* **contrite** *in spirit, and trembles at my word.'"* Remaining contrite will help you remain in God's presence and will allow His love to continue to be built in your heart.

There are some specific things God placed within you at the creation of your life as described in Psalm 139:13, *"For you created my inmost being; you knit me together in my mother's womb."* God created your inmost being and brought you to life. He placed your heart within you which is a deposit from God. It determined who you are and who you were intended to be. 2 Corinthians 4:6 says this, *"For God, who said, "Let light shine out of darkness," made His light shine in our hearts to give us the light of the knowledge of the glory of God in the face of Christ."* The light shining in darkness is the creative power of God to illuminate your heart to the need for Him.

This is the reason for Romans 1:20 which says *"For since the creation of the world God's invisible qualities – His eternal power and divine nature – have been clearly seen, being understood from what has been made, so that men are without excuse."* What was started at the creation of the world? Life!! God created life and breathed life into man and at that moment He put something deep within man so that man would know God through creation. He wants us to find Him so He created us with a void that would draw us back to Him. The problem came when sin entered man's heart and he tried to fill that void with things he could see and touch. For many, the void designed to beckon us to God is now silenced altogether!

I heard a story about a lady who lived directly adjacent to a railroad track. She had lived in the same home for 30+ years. As she and her pastor were having coffee and talking one afternoon a train rolled through and scared the pastor half-to-death. The lady was unmoved by the commotion. As the pastor calmed himself, he quickly asked how she could ever put up with such a noise. She responded with this, "If you just quit listening long enough, you stop hearing it." She may have been talking about a train, but the same applies to your heart; your spiritual heart to be exact.

When you were just a child you acted and reacted from your heart. You didn't know any better. You said what came to mind, because what came to your mind was directly from your heart.

You lived out wild adventures in your backyard, because something was beckoning you to something bigger than yourself. You made a parachute out of a bed sheet and jumped off the garage roof because you wanted to know what it was like to be a soldier leaping out of a plane. You set up booby traps throughout the woods behind your house because you wanted to protect the family. You imagined how you would one day rescue a beautiful girl in a heroic adventure.

As a little girl you daydreamed about what romantic adventures you would find. You twirled around in your princess dress imagining what it would be like on your wedding day to dance with the man of your dreams. You took special care of your dolls and imagined what it would be like to be a mother. You gave your friends hugs when they were crying and you tried to take care of them the best you could. You sat and drew pictures for hours of the horse you would one day ride through the meadows.

Your heart was the source of all these possible adventures.

Why did our hearts take us to all these places? Because God wants each of us to dream, and His dream for each of us is that we would share in His love and live out His adventure for our lives! He placed those desires in your heart because you are the only person that will ever have the heart God specifically gave to you. You are the only one who will ever see Him from your perspective. Your perspective of beauty and mystery is as unique to you as the fingerprint on your finger. Your idea of adventure cannot be compared to another's because God wants you to experience the specific adventure He wrote for you and for no one else. You are the only one who will ever be able to find your way home to Him the way He wants you to!! It is so important that you see how much the Father loves you.

Interestingly, humans tend to spend most of their time wondering if the people around them, the ones they care about and esteem, see things the way they do. The subconscious question revolves around acceptance and rejection. People tend to get dressed in the hopes that their clothes are acceptable. They tend to desire a relationship with someone that others would also think is attractive. They even stop themselves from sharing significant experiences because they fear others will view them as silly or stupid. People spend their whole lives trying to view beauty and mystery from the same perspective, but then judge one another on the inability to come to a unanimous decision. Yet, because of the uniqueness created in every person, beauty and mystery is not supposed to be governed by majority vote.

God created your heart specifically for the beauty of His choosing, and an adventure that He wants you to live. Our God is so great, that no two people will ever be attracted to the very same things nor will any two people ever live out the same adventures. Everyone has received their unique desires from the Creator.

Vulnerable

Your Genesis Moment is critical to your heart being able to dream again. Only then can you love God with all of our heart, soul, mind, and strength. God's creative power to heal your heart will release childlike faith and wonder. Jesus said in Mark 10:15, *"I tell you the truth, anyone who will not receive the kingdom of God like a little child will never enter it."* In the process of being re-made you had to go back to your childhood and commit to the pain that you endured and trust Jesus for healing. As we have already covered, the reason most attacks are effective is because children are vulnerable. Childlike love and heartfelt reactions equate to vulnerability. God wants us to once again be vulnerable because that is where genuine love thrives.

A free heart can dream because it's your heart that feeds your soul, your mind, and your body. One effect of the captive heart in our world today is people living with withered hearts.

When a heart is set free to be vulnerable again, it releases dreams within the soul through your unique personality. Without freedom in your heart, your soul is afraid to dream because of the potential for rejection, just like the pain you first received that started the captivity.

Now as dreams are released in your soul, your mind is engaged to think new thoughts, and make new decisions based upon your dreams. God created you to be a creator – you were made in His image. Without a free heart, and without dreams, your mind was convinced its only job was to survive by protecting what remained, so your decisions have all been self-centered.

Once your heart and soul engage your mind in childlike wonder, your body will be the means by which you will carry out those dreams. This process of spiritual growth circles back and fills your heart with more of God's love as you watch Him work in and through your life. Without God's creation power to free your heart, your body, your mind, and your soul, they will all work together tirelessly at securing your protection and strengthen the trap. Ultimately that self-protection will wither your heart which God intended to flourish.

Pain is viewed as punishment. This is why the Bible says in 1 John 4:18-19, *"there is no fear in love, but perfect love casts out fear. For fear has to do with punishment, and whoever fears has not been perfected in love. We love because he first loved us."* Perfect love is God's love. The antidote for fear is not courage. It is love. Love is the result of your Genesis Moment. Until perfect love comes, fear continues to rule, and when fear rules in your heart protection from pain is your only motivator. It may sound scary right now to become vulnerable once again, but your vulnerability will ultimately mean perfect love.

Dreams were erased by pain just as your heart was beckoning you to a life filled with genuine love and adventure. You were vulnerable and the enemy took advantage. By recognizing the source of your wounds and acknowledging them through your autobiography, you are telling the Lord that you commit to Him as your healer. Your healing is not possible in your own effort. You must commit and submit to His power to be healed.

Pain

Put the responsibility for your pain where it belongs, on the enemy. God does not give His children a spirit of fear. Fear is Satan's tool to bring destruction. Remember, his only tactics are to hurt us where we want to do something, be somebody, or have something. No matter what form the arrow took, it was sent to make sure that one of your emotional needs was unmet, and in so doing caused you deep pain. Those wounds came straight from Satan's bow in the form of flaming arrows, and when they hit their mark, they shook you to the core with searing pain.

"A Heart of Stone!"
Once in pain, we would never be the same.
From whence came this pain?
I must be to blame!
It's here now to stay and stain.
Where Love was meant to untame,
Only Pain will Reign!

The arrows came through those you valued the most, the people you believed defined life to its full extent, and so the hurt was real, settling in your heart. You have to know that those people were not the source of your wounds; they were only the enemy's bow. The source is the enemy himself. In fact he has done such an outstanding job of putting men and women in bondage that his work is minimal as the new generations appear. People who are in bondage carry out his work by putting their children unknowingly in the same bondage, and so the cycle continues in destructive strength. It was the people you trusted the most to help you live out your dreams that were actually used to quench them. Your dreams were lost and your romances died. You were told to grow up and stop being a child, to be more mature, more like them, when in fact it was not like them you should have become at all.

You may be asking the question, "How could this happen?"

The answer is simple; the Truth had not yet been revealed. You were left without God's truth to filter out the lies you were hearing. As the Bible says, all have sinned, all have fallen short of the Glory of God and until the day God's Truth is revealed, lies are believed. Romans 5:12 says, *"Therefore, just as sin entered the world through one man, and death through sin and in this way death came to all men, because all sinned."*

Sinners do not have the Truth to use as a filter against the damaging blows dealt to them by the people they value the most. Satan rejoices every time a child's spiritual heart is attacked. He knows his lies are effective in children who have not yet received the revelation of God's Truth. Children, without a defense, can only look to those, by whom life has been shaped, for the "norm." They view these people as great and good; therefore, any negativity they encounter is perceived to be their own fault. In sin they wrestle with the fear and the pain that enters their hearts, and

116

they know nothing else but to create their own interpretation of the pain they have been dealt.

John Eldredge and Brent Curtis point out in *Sacred Romance* a quote by Julia Gatta, "Experience, no matter how accurately understood, can never furnish its own interpretation."[xii] A child is left to interpret their experience only by bouncing it off what they know to be true, and unfortunately without the Truth of Jesus Christ all explanations fall short. They bounce experiences off ideals. They believe that their parents are the truth, that their friends are the truth, that their role models are the truth. Wrong. No one is the Truth but Jesus Christ. Through ideals children begin a self-destructive view of life in which they tell themselves that the love that they have received is the most they will ever get. At that moment, children believe lies about themselves and the world they live in, and the enemy takes hold as he watches the bondage begin.

Once you started believing the lies that these various unmet emotional needs were telling you, you fell further away from reality. Just because you experienced pain, doesn't mean your emotional needs went away. In fact, they only became stronger. Unmet emotional needs give birth to stronger emotional needs as the child grasps for anything to try and meet their own needs. Experience has taught them that their ideals cannot meet their needs, so they take matters into their own hands. Once you took matters into your own hands, your coping mechanisms began to form.

In my case, I tried to find a way to make myself feel loved because I believed that I was unlovable. My need to be loved only increased as I believed the lie that I didn't deserve to be loved. Eventually I created a fantasy world that I thought would satisfy my longings, if only temporarily, and that became my addiction. I developed my coping mechanisms to protect myself from the possible pain of not being loved. Simply put, I was afraid of not being loved. Whenever situations would arise where I saw the possibility that my emotional needs were not going to be met, I would quickly grab my coping mechanism to try and avoid the inevitable pain. Fear of emotional pain kept me in this bondage and caused me to go back time and time again to the fantasy world I created where I would get temporary relief in self-indulgence. In my mind, the self-indulgence, although destructive, still felt better than the possible pain.

The enemy holds you captive to your coping mechanisms by telling you that it's the best you are going to get out of this life. The coping mechanism then becomes a prison that traps the heart. This trap is like sealing your heart inside a titanium vault. No matter which direction longings come at you or life comes at you, anytime it gets close to the heart, you quickly grab your coping mechanisms to defend against any more possible pain. But unfortunately, every successful deflection of pain only serves to strengthen the vault around your heart. With the enemy's help you can possibly imprison your heart to the point that you lose feeling all together as you simply strive to survive. Through your coping mechanisms you become the warden of your own imprisoned heart. An imprisoned heart is faintly beating in your chest, but it doesn't call out, it doesn't dream, it doesn't cry, because it only knows the prison.

Though you didn't know at the time, pain and your desire to escape it is what put you in bondage. Today, the sin pattern you are walking away from was the prison that held your heart. It had become such a part of your life, that you may have mistaken the imprisoned heart as your identity. Even God's beckoning call to your heart was perceived as potential pain. Your heart couldn't

118

hear Him because it was locked up. When you felt an emotional void, or you were tired, lonely, discouraged, despairing, or impatient you found yourself running immediately to your coping mechanisms.

Even if you had spent months avoiding your coping mechanisms, eventually you fell back into the same pattern. Why? Because your heart still hadn't been set free. Ephesians 4:18 says, *"They are darkened in their understanding and separated from the life of God because of the ignorance that is in them due to the **harden**ing of their hearts."* An imprisoned heart is a hard heart, and maybe until now, you didn't know what was happening. Without a free heart you cannot fulfill the greatest commandment to love the Lord your God with all your heart, with all your soul, with all your mind, and with all your strength. Nor can you fulfill the second which is like the first; to love your neighbor as yourself.

But this is the prison that you are leaving behind. You are stepping forward in faith with the Lord Jesus Christ as you continue to hold to His commands. You are now in a vulnerable place, but it is the vulnerable heart that God requires and holds close to His own. Isaiah 57:16 says, *"For thus says the One who is high and lifted up, who inhabits eternity, whose name is Holy: 'I dwell in the high and holy place, and also with him who is of a contrite and lowly spirit, to revive the spirit of the lowly, and to revive the heart of the contrite."* As you rest in Christ let His voice beckon you all the more into His divine and majestic intimacy. He longs to hold you close and to be held in highest regard by the beautiful and adventurous heart within you.

True Story

One of the young men who walked through this process has given me permission to share his story with you, but for the sake of his privacy we will call him Johnny. His story is about a heart that was attacked and nearly destroyed early in his life, only to have been revived by Jesus' creation power in his own Genesis Moment.

Johnny was born when his mother was only 16 years old. She had no idea about raising a child, as she was still one herself. She prolifically used and abused drugs and alcohol. Johnny's biological father was cut from the same cloth and also used and abused drugs and alcohol. Johnny's earliest memories were shrouded in clouds of smoke and smells of alcohol and vomit. His first memory of why he existed came when he was told that his life was a mistake. His parents were inconvenienced by his birth, and all he heard about was how much he had cost them. No matter what problems arose between his parents, he was blamed. He learned at a very early age what it meant to be angry and to fight as he witnessed countless battles between his parents. When they would fight he knew it was only a matter of time before one of them would take out their frustrations on him. He would get beaten by his father, or verbally abused by his mother. Often times he would have nothing to do with the issues, but by default, he was blamed. Maybe you can relate to Johnny.

Johnny also learned about sex too early in life. Whenever his mother would break up with his father, Johnny remembers countless men that would parade through his house and through his mother. Dealing with sex, drugs, and alcohol became normal for Johnny. Like any other little boy, he was born with a heart designed by God for God's purpose, and yet the enemy had done such a great job in his parents that they were destroying Johnny's heart before it ever had a chance to live. He wanted to feel loved. He wanted to be someone special. He wanted to have what he thought all the other kids had, a family that loved him. He wanted someone to care about him, to take care of him, and who would be proud of him. Instead every one of his emotional needs went unmet as he was being devastated emotionally and physically. He also had a little sister who he worked hard to protect, but being the girl, she was spared the kind of treatment that he endured.

Johnny finally found one person to love him. A waitress at the local bar that his parents frequented was kind enough to make Shirley Temples for him and his sister. They would sit with her and drink their sprites while mom and dad would get drunk and rowdy. The waitress would bring them food and give them quarters to play pinball. Finally, Johnny had discovered someone that showed interest in him, someone that would take some of the burden off of his heart, but as quickly as love came, it left. Johnny learned later that his friend had been fired from the bar because someone accused her of molesting him and his sister. This was yet another spiritual heart attack for him, a devastating blow. Satan wanted Johnny to be destroyed and so he attacked the one person that was filling his heart with love.

During his elementary school years Johnny found himself with a rare nerve condition that prevented his nerve endings in his colon from signaling his brain when he needed to go to the bathroom. Because he had no ability to feel the urge to go, he would do one of two things. He would either hold it too long and become severely constipated, or he would be unable to hold it back and soil his pants.

As an elementary student, it only took one of these experiences to cause him to be an outcast. But unfortunately the frequency of those experiences left him with no hope for love. He always stunk, his clothes were always dirty, and all the kids made fun of him. In his own heart, he believed that he was disgusting and unlovable. When the constipation would become too great, an excruciating pain would fill his stomach. Four times he was admitted to the ER to have his stomach pumped as a result of this condition. Each time he would cry out for his father, but no one was there. He was left alone to face his battle.

He would just sit and cry, believing every lie that the enemy was telling him. He heard over and over in his heart that he just wasn't important enough to have someone there to help him.

If only he could have known that Jesus was right there at his side holding his hand as Isaiah 41:13 says, *"For I am the LORD, your God, who takes hold of your right hand and says to you, Do not fear; I will help you."* This is one of the truths that Johnny holds tightly today after realizing Jesus' love for him, but as we mentioned before, without the Truth, as a young boy Johnny was left to fend for himself.

When Johnny's father would eventually see him, he would blame Johnny for the problem and beat him severely for doing such a dumb thing. His father's verbal and physical abuse translated to Johnny that it was his fault. As if all the other attacks he suffered weren't enough, this one came with devastating power capable of killing the heart within him.

As Johnny grew up he started developing a relationship with his grandfather, Pop, who showed him healthy love. Pop always told him stories of the war and told Johnny what a man he would be one day. Pop became a very special part of Johnny's life. Pop often talked about the Navy SEAL's. Hearing how his grandfather spoke of the SEAL's, Johnny began to dream of the acceptance and importance that kind of honor would bring into his own life if he were to one day achieve the goal of being a SEAL. It quickly became his dream of "being". But as Johnny's relationship was growing with Pop, another arrow struck. Pop was diagnosed with lung cancer from the Agent Orange in Vietnam. Johnny's hero and the only one who seemed to love him, was now dying and would soon leave just like everyone else. It felt like more than Johnny could handle.

The call eventually came that Pop had very little time left. Pop had saved some money to buy a plane ticket for Johnny, and he rushed back to see his hero for the last time. As he sat beside the hospital bed he said, "Grandpop – I love you, please don't leave, I'm scared." Pop squeezed his hand tightly as a tear rolled down his cheek. That that was the last thing Pop ever did. He died holding Johnny's hand. Johnny was only 12 years old.

Three years later, he was fast asleep one night in his bed at his mother's house only be to awoken by two very obese women tying him to the bed. They proceeded after tying him up to rape him. His mother had sold her son for drugs. The innocence lost could never be restored. The next day he turned 16 and left his mother's house never to return.

An empty soul set out into the world at the age of 16, a broken little boy left to fend for himself. Johnny tried the best he could with what he had. After leaving his mother's care he started boxing and eventually became a golden gloves winner. He was a superior athlete with the determination to succeed that far exceeded the other kids. He was being driven to defy all the pain he felt in his heart. Yet all the pain also made him a fighter outside of the boxing gym. He would often fight and find himself in trouble with the police.

Around this same time, his father attacked him again and in a fit of rage he told Johnny that he would NEVER be someone special. The words echoed through Johnny's ears and heart like a mortar. Never be someone special???!!! Again a lie from the enemy surfaced which Johnny chose to believe because he still lacked the revealed truth of God. Those words shaped everything Johnny did from that point on. One day he saw a poster during a recruiting video for the SEAL's which said "Be Someone Special!" Remembering back to his times with Pop, Johnny grabbed onto the idea of becoming someone special and signed up to be a Navy Seal.

He set out on a journey with a former Navy SEAL coach named Cory, to prepare for his training, and quickly his coach recognized Johnny's superior ability. He was recognized for his grit, determination, and psychotic ability to push past the limits that made all the others quit. Cory worked with him constantly for two years. During this time, Cory talked of the love that Christ offers to us all and invited Johnny to church with him. Jesus saved Johnny one night in a Bible study at the pastor's house and for the first time he felt love like he had never felt. He accepted the gift of salvation that God offered through Jesus' blood. But that didn't mean that his heart was free from all the pain and damage he carried.

As Johnny excelled in SEAL training, he broke multiple records, and rose to the top of his class. He completed the feared hell week and only had one person attend his graduation; a girl he had been seeing in high school. She was the only one who cared enough to be present during a defining moment in Johnny's life. Again the lies struck.

Just as he was to be shipped off as a SEAL news came back from administration that there was a problem with his paperwork. Johnny was discharged from the SEAL team because of an administrative error regarding a past arrest on his record while he was a minor. Johnny was devastated. He moved back north and became a personal trainer and got away from Christian fellowship. He was battling with all the lies in his heart and barely hanging onto life. He was only getting out of life what he thought he could get, protection was his only option. He buried it once again under all the other wreckage.

Hope

Knowing none of this at the time of our meeting, God blessed me by allowing me to meet Johnny. We met at the gym and immediately became friends. God placed Johnny in my life for a specific reason and today I am humbled and honored to call him my friend. I have witnessed this damaged little boy be transformed from a kid who was afraid to give someone a birthday card because of his fear of rejection, to a man who was able to pray and thank Jesus in front of hundreds of people for his new life.

Johnny experienced his own Genesis Moment and his heart was transformed and set free from all the lies and damage that were once his identity. He was finally able to begin living the life God called him to live. Johnny is a living example of a heart set free to be loved by God and to love God as He intends.

Johnny's story should not only break your heart for all the children that are suffering a similar fate today, but it should also give you hope that your story is not too great to overcome. Our God rules and reigns perfectly and He will heal anyone who is willing to commit to the pain and give it to Him. He will take all that pain and wipe it away replacing it with the abundant life of beauty and mystery found in Jesus Christ.

Assignment

Before you move on to the next chapter and after you have read your autobiography to your team there is another exercise that is critical to helping you replace the lies with truth. I know God is already placing within you a renewed spirit and a desire for Him, but there may be remnants of lies still tucked away in your heart. One of the ways you can bring those lies into the light is to create two separate lists of outcomes – those outcomes you hoped to experience and those outcomes you actually experienced while acting out in your coping mechanisms. The first list is the desired outcomes.

Desired outcomes are the results you hoped to achieve or the feelings you hoped to feel through your coping mechanisms. If your coping mechanism is sexual addiction the outcomes you hope for can be things like excitement, sexual fulfillment, satisfaction, acceptance, significance, and security. Depending on your coping mechanism the list may look very similar or it may look completely different. List any emotional, physical, or psychological outcomes you hoped to achieve.

Once the first list is complete then go back and write out the list of the actual outcomes that were the result of your coping mechanism. Often these are things like resentment, guilt, frustration, separation from God, alienation from others, greater longing for security and significance, shame, etc. The list of the actual outcomes versus the outcomes you hoped to achieve will shine light on the fact that your coping mechanism never brought fulfillment. True contentment is only found in Jesus Christ and the relationship He offers. Be sure and read your lists to someone on your team and express to them and to the Lord your renouncement of those lies. Declare the truth out loud.

One other thing you should do with this list is look in the Bible and find passages in God's Word that replace the lies you believed with His Truth. Write these truths down in your journal and read over them often. You cannot just sweep your heart clean; you must also fill your heart with the Truth of God's Word.

In the next chapter we will look at the change from the heart of stone into the heart of flesh. We will see how the diagram you studied in Chapter 4 is transformed by God's power into the life giving flow of righteousness that Isaiah 58 speaks of.

Reflections:

1. Have you started to recall the adventures you hoped to live? Write down what those dreams were and also write out some of your dreams that you have right now.

2. Write out 3 specific ways you can increase your vulnerability with Jesus and with others.

3. Write a short paragraph of how Johnny's story related to your own and thank the Lord that He is able to overcome and transform your life.

Chapter 7

A Heart of Flesh

Johnny's story is a stark reminder of our society's current condition. Every day children are being born into families just like Johnny's. Every day, every hour, children are suffering the blows of unmet emotional needs, and hearts are being taken prisoner. Yet, it is God's will that all would come to repentance and that all would be free to love Him as He intends. My prayer is that you are continuing to walk obediently in Jesus' commands, not just by religious rule following, but abiding in Jesus and beholding Him. Are you walking in compassion every day, with every chance you get? Do you care about the souls of the people around you, or are you still focusing on your own problems and pain and ignoring the people around you?

In this chapter we want to look at the way the heart of stone becomes the heart of flesh. A heart of flesh is one that has the transforming love of Jesus Christ pulsing through it. Only Jesus' love placed in us makes us capable of compassion and care for other people. As we have covered, the heart is easily deceived and the reality of genuine Godly love is often absent when people search for "love" as only the world gives.

Seeing the Pitch

This morning I met with a young man I'll call Tom. Tom has been a professional baseball player for the past few years. He came to me this morning after our Tuesday night Bible study and wanted to know more about this trap around his heart. He wants to find his identity in God, not in baseball. He said to me, "I know I'm not ready for the big leagues, because I still find my identity in baseball, and even if I got there I know I would still not be happy." He was exactly right. What an encouragement it was to hear that he wanted to be whole with God before He did anything else in his life. This is my prayer for you, that you will keep speaking the truth into your own life and that your Genesis Moment is taking you deeper into the love that is offered in Jesus Christ.

Tom has done what so many of us do with the things in life by which we identify ourselves; he created a romance out of baseball. Baseball is beautiful to him – well only when he is winning. Baseball is adventurous to him because he never knows what will come next. Baseball gives him a chance to be part of something much bigger than himself, especially when he pitches a winning game. But his romance has a flaw – his lover is imperfect. When identity is dependent on the outcome then the beauty of winning the game can also turn to the ugliness of a loss, and the impact is devastating. The mystery and wonder of what will happen next in the big game is destroyed and lost when the losing pitch is thrown and the team is let down. His romance cannot offer security because it's an imperfect lover.

Like the rest of us, Tom experienced pain during his emotional development early in life. He was "pitched" a functional identity by which the world would come to see him succeed. The lie he believed, because he heard it from his dad, who he valued above everyone else, was that love would only come through success in baseball. Again that was the lie he began to tell himself. The losses would devastate him, not only because he let the team down, but because he felt unworthy to be loved after losing. It would cause him to recede into depression and trap his heart further in the prison of hiding, drinking, or sleeping with women.

The imperfect lover left him with a sense of gratification only when he won. Winning brought an outpouring of love (worldly recognition and attention which was masquerading as love), and so it became more and more necessary to win. The desire to be loved fueled his desire to win. But because the loss of love was attached to the loss of the game, one loss would erase all the wins.

Satan wanted Tom to believe that winning equals love because then Tom will always get hurt because no one wins every time. Satan wants to see Tom hurt and depressed and destroyed, and so he keeps telling him he must win! Even when Tom loses the game he still seeks a high and so he turns to his coping mechanisms. Even when he would sleep with a woman, it was all about the score, meaning her perception of his performance. Even in his sins he felt that he must win.

Tom was trapped by the identity that others gave him through his success in baseball. He views the world from judgmental eyes. He was judged in the past by the performance he offered and so the assumptions continue that he will always be judged. He is trapped under this weight of possible judgment by fear – a fear that he will not be accepted for what he is and what he does.

In order to never reach the pain of the judgment he must head off every possible avenue by grabbing onto his coping mechanisms. He acts out based only on what he thinks others are thinking. In this way he can escape the pain of their judgment by foregoing the interaction altogether. But as he runs from the possible judgment he also runs from the possible love. The further he runs, the more love he needs, and the only way he knows how to get it is to cope but in reality he never finds it.

As he copes with his fears he traps his heart even further. It's the fear of judgment and rejection that keeps him from knowing real love. This is exactly what people do with the emotional pain in their lives – they have a fear so strong that they could get hurt again that they run and hide in their coping mechanisms and starve themselves from the love they truly need. God wants you to feel His love intimately, compassionately, self-sacrificially, wholly and perfectly. If you haven't yet come to experience God's love this way, you have probably been too busy running from your fears.

Facing the Mountain

Someone who was seeking their own Genesis Moment that we'll call Lori said to me one day, "I don't want to hurt anymore." My response, which I believe came from the Holy Spirit was, "Yes you do!" Now before you think we are supposed to seek out pain, let me further explain my response.

Early in her journey toward the Genesis Moment she still believed the lies that Satan was telling her about how the pain would come. The fears were piling up and instead of wanting to continue, retreating again seemed to be the best option to avoid any potential pain. She needed a reminder of why the search for freedom began in the first place. The pursuit began so she could be free from the pain her father had inflicted on her heart by his inability to meet her emotional needs. "I want to live," is how she put it. She wanted freedom from the cycles of bad relationships that continued to plague her life and she wanted to be able to have and love a family one day. She needed to be reminded that she wanted to LIVE.

In order to live, you must be willing to die. To feel alive you must be willing to take a risk and put forth the effort that is often painful in the moment. No one who sits in safety all their life feels the rush of barely escaping death. People do not climb Mount Everest because it's a hard mountain to climb. They climb Mount Everest because in success they feel alive, more alive than ever before because they have escaped death. They must be willing to die and even endure some pain before even beginning the adventure.

So it is with us as spiritual beings. To love and feel loved you must be willing to be hurt. Only a heart of flesh is both loving and lovable, but it is also vulnerable to potential pain. The beautiful thing about the potential pain we talk about is that the Lord Almighty promises to be our protector. Isaiah 41:13 says *"For I am the LORD, your God, who takes hold of your right hand and says to you, Do not fear; I will help you."* Nothing that comes our way will hurt because God becomes our perfect lover. He is perfect to protect and when we find our value, our identity, and our worth in Him there is nothing that can hurt us.

To really live and love, you will have to be willing to face potential hurt, just remember you can place it on Jesus. Romans 15:3 says, *"For Christ did not please himself, but as it is written, 'The reproaches of those who reproached you fell on me.'"*

Perfect Lover

God - our perfect Lover - is perfect in the three necessary elements of any relationship. God is perfect in his communication. He has written us a love letter called the Bible, so that we may know all about Him and how to please Him. He has also sent us his Spirit so that we may perceive the things of God to know Him supernaturally. 1 Corinthians 2:9-10 says *"However, as it is written: "No eye has seen, no ear has heard, no mind has conceived what God has prepared for those who love him" but God has revealed it to us by his Spirit."* God's Spirit communicates with those who believe so that they can know Him and what He has prepared for them!

God is also perfect in Service! Every morning God provides us with sunlight. Every second God provides us with oxygen to keep us alive. Every millisecond God holds the fabric of our body together with Laminin (google it if you've never heard of it) so that we do not disintegrate. Without God serving us constantly we would cease to exist. Isaiah 40:28 says *"Do you not know? Have you not heard? The LORD is the everlasting God, the Creator of the ends of the earth. He will not grow tired or weary, and his understanding no one can fathom."* He serves us without stopping.

God is perfect in Intimacy! God the Father, The Holy Spirit, and Jesus were perfectly intimate before the creation of man. They glorify one another and through that glory fill each other with love. As the very nature of God, the Trinity is love according to 1 John 4:16 *"And so we know and rely on the love God has for us. God is love. Whoever lives in love lives in God, and God in him."* Man was created out of this perfect intimacy in the image of perfect intimacy and with the need for perfect intimacy. Often this beckoning of the human heart for intimacy is mistaken for the fears of pain we become so accustomed to fending off. This search for intimacy placed in our heart by a sovereign God is then headed off by our coping mechanisms because we do not recognize where it is coming from – love.

How is God perfectly intimate? Because He is always present. Whenever you call out to Him, He is there. He never sleeps and He never slumbers. He never grows tired or weary. He is omnipresent, meaning He is everywhere all the time. Colossians 1:17 says, *"He is before all things, and in Him all things hold together."* Not only is He always present, but to the believer He is residing within.

The two become one flesh at the point of salvation. God deposits His mind, the Holy Spirit, into the believer so that each one of us can have the consciousness of God at all times. 2 Corinthians 1:22 says, *"He anointed us, [22] set his seal of ownership on us, and put his Spirit in our hearts as a deposit, guaranteeing what is to come."* Sex between husband and wife is the representation of the indwelling of the Holy Spirit in the believer. Therefore, sex within the marriage bed becomes a picture of your salvation experience every time it is experienced. He gives us the greatest physical satisfaction to represent the greatest spiritual intimacy. This is the intimate God who loves us. Song of Solomon was not just written as a racy book in the Bible. It was written to give us a picture of what kind of relationship God wants with each of us spiritually.

Triune Sufficiency

God is also Abba Father – or Daddy. Romans 8:15 says this *"For you did not receive a spirit that makes you a slave again to fear, but you received the Spirit of sonship. And by him we cry, "Abba, Father."* God is our Daddy and ready to help us in our time of need. The more we cry out to God for our needs the more love He lavishes upon us. James 4:8 says, *"Draw near unto me and I will draw near unto you."* God wants you to come to him and let Him be your protector.

God is also the Holy Spirit – or the Mind of God as we talked about when we discussed the Trinity. Acts 15:8 says, *"God, who knows the heart, showed that he accepted them by giving the Holy Spirit to them, just as he did to us."* The Holy Spirit fills three important roles in our lives.

The first is as a teacher. He knows the mind of God and therefore supernaturally allows us to be enlightened to God's wisdom through Scripture. He also intercedes on our behalf to the Father because of our inability to know how or what to pray.

Secondly, the Holy Spirit is our greatest source of encouragement. He comforts us when we walk in righteousness and obey the Truth of God's word.

And thirdly, His role in our life is judge. He convicts us when we are stepping toward something we shouldn't. He enlightens us in these three roles as we need to be enlightened. Ephesians 1:17 says, *"I keep asking that the God of our Lord Jesus Christ, the glorious Father, may give you the Spirit of wisdom and revelation, so that you may know him better."* And yet, there are so many other ways the Holy Spirit will manifest Himself in our lives if only we will continue in belief.

God is also Jesus – the flesh of God, the Logos, the Word, The Way the Truth and the Life. Jesus is my brother. Hebrews 2:11 says this, *"Both the One who makes men holy and those who are made holy are of the same family. So Jesus is not ashamed to call them brothers. He says, 'I will declare Your name to my brothers; in the presence of the congregation I will sing Your praises.'"* Vs 14-15 says, *"Since the children have flesh and blood, He too shared in their humanity so that by His death He might destroy Him who holds the power of death – that is, the*

*devil – and free those who all their lives were held in slavery by
their fear of death."*

As my brother I view Jesus as a strong man, powerful in
all He does. He stands at my side with eyes of fire and fists of
steel ready to fight for me at any moment. The flames of
righteousness surround Him and cover Him and drip off Him onto
the ground. Any enemy who attacks us will be devoured by the
Power of the Cross. Jesus is a mighty warrior, death could not
handle Him and the grave could not hold Him. He is our King –
because of our love for the King we will serve Him as His loyal
bondservants. He is our daily bread, and He is our spring of living
water, He is our help when we are weak, and He is our intercessor.
Oh, He is so much more to us, but this book cannot contain that
length of description.

Freedom's Protection

As you can see, contentedness is found in the relational
roles being met by the *"I AM!"* How do we love Him? We
commit! Loving is committing to obedience. <u>This is where your
follow through in the practical steps of seeking freedom are met
by His supernatural creation power that sets you free.</u> Love is an
action tied to an emotion. God is Love. He asks for your actions
in the form of obedience. Obedience is the proof of your love to
Him through every day decisions. He promised that your
obedience will be blessed by His love being poured out on you
supernaturally.

The simple act of writing your autobiography and reading
it aloud to your team was actually a step of obedience and love for
God. God wants <u>you</u> to know that you are committed to what you
are asking for, and in admitting and committing by writing out

your painful past and reading it aloud, you showed that your true desire is to realize your own Genesis Moment and be set free to live and love. God sees that commitment in your life when you are obedient to His Word and He promises healing.

Psalm 32 describes this healing:

"Blessed is the one whose transgression is forgiven, whose sin is covered. Blessed is the man against whom the Lord counts no iniquity, and in whose spirit there is no deceit. For when I kept silent, my bones wasted away through my groaning all day long. For day and night your hand was heavy upon me; my strength was dried up as by the heat of summer. I acknowledged my sin to you, and I did not cover my iniquity; I said, 'I will confess my transgressions to the Lord,' and you forgave the iniquity of my sin. Selah Therefore let everyone who is godly offer prayer to you at a time when you may be found; surely in the rush of great waters, they shall not reach him. You are a hiding place for me; you preserve me from trouble; you surround me with shouts of deliverance. Selah I will instruct you and teach you in the way you should go; I will counsel you with my eye upon you. Be not like a horse or a mule, without understanding, which must be curbed with bit and bridle, or it will not stay near you. Many are the sorrows of the wicked, but the steadfast love surrounds the one who trusts in the Lord. Be glad in the Lord, and rejoice, O righteous, and shout for joy, all you upright in heart!"

Always remember how your compassionate obedience plays a significant role in your healing. Isaiah 58:6-9 as we reviewed before says, *""Is not this the kind of fasting (*obedience*) I have chosen: to loose the chains of injustice and untie the cords of the yoke, to set the oppressed free and break every yoke? Is it not to share your food with the hungry and to provide the poor wanderer with shelter— when you see the naked, to clothe him,* *and not to turn away from your own flesh and blood? Then your light will break forth like the dawn, and your healing will quickly appear; then your righteousness will go before you, and the glory of the LORD will be your rear guard. Then you will call, and the LORD will answer; you will cry for help, and he will say: Here am I.*"

God seeks people of compassion who desire what God desires. God is the God of compassion. James 2:14-17 say this, "*What good is it, my brothers, if a man claims to have faith but has no deeds? Can such faith save him? [15]Suppose a brother or sister is without clothes and daily food. [16]If one of you says to him, "Go, I wish you well; keep warm and well fed," but does nothing about his physical needs, what good is it? [17]In the same way, faith by itself, if it is not accompanied by action, is dead.*" God makes it plain that it is compassion He desires from those who love Him.

1 John 3:16-24 says, "*This is how we know what love is: Jesus Christ laid down his life for us. And we ought to lay down our lives for our brothers. [17]If anyone has material possessions and sees his brother in need but has no pity on him, how can the love of God be in him? [18]Dear children, let us not love with words or tongue but with actions and in truth. [19]This then is how we know that we belong to the truth, and how we set our hearts at rest in his presence [20]whenever our hearts condemn us. For God is greater than our hearts, and he knows everything. Dear friends, if our hearts do not condemn us, we have confidence before God [22]and receive from him anything we ask, because we obey his commands and do what pleases him. [23]And this is his command: to believe in the name of his Son, Jesus Christ, and to love one another as he commanded us. [24]Those who obey his commands live in him, and he in them. And this is how we know that he lives in us: We know it by the Spirit he gave us.*"

There is only one way to love God; you must live out your life in compassion toward others. God promises healing in Isaiah 58. He requires your obedience in compassion. Only He knows if you will truly lay down your life for others, but with each act of obedience in your life, He is proving His power to overcome what the devil tried to do. God loves you enough to convince you of how much you love Him. God's wisdom has provided for your healing through the process of removing your eyes and your focus from your own problems and placing your eyes and your focus on the needs of others.

Your acts of obedience and love, born out of a motive to love God, guarantee the fulfillment of His Word, because He cannot lie. Healing is dependent upon His promise, not upon your actions. Yet when your actions align with His promise you will experience the fulfillment of His Word.

When you hold out the broken pieces of your heart to Him, commit to the pain and fear, believe His truths alone, and act out of a heart of compassion, *your light will break forth like the dawn and your healing will come quickly!!!!* God will not delay in setting you free from the *chains of injustice and untying the cords of the yoke, setting the oppressed free and breaking every yoke!* That is how much God loves you and that is your Genesis Moment.

When you are set free, *your righteousness will go before you, and the glory of the LORD will be your rear guard.* God is saying that healing is granting you a free heart that can love him and is free to be loved by Him. Out of that free heart will come forth righteousness in the form of your actions fueled by His power. He will become your rear guard, meaning God has got your back. This is how God protects those who belong to Him. That is a heart of flesh.

139

The Free Heart

The diagram we looked at in the earlier chapters as the trapped heart is now transformed from a heart of stone to a heart of flesh. In this diagram it is evident that the coping mechanisms are gone and that true love in your heart is the result of your heart's freedom.

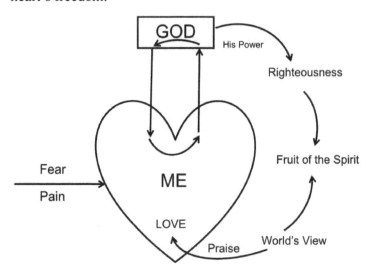

Romans 6:17-18 "We have become slaves to righteousness...

No Coping Mechanisms

As you can see in the diagram above, the relationship to God has been restored by the freedom experienced in fulfilling Isaiah 58:6-9, discovering your pain, identifying your coping mechanisms, confessing your sins through your autobiography, and replacing the lies with Truth. Compare this diagram of freedom to the diagram of the trapped heart on the next page.

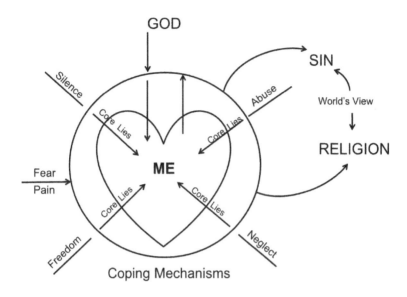

Coping Mechanisms

You can see in the diagram of the free heart that the arrow returning from your heart to God is no longer broken. The reestablishment of your heart's first response back to God is explained by Isaiah 58:8 which says, *"Then shall your light break forth like the dawn, and your healing shall spring up speedily; your righteousness shall go before you; the glory of the Lord shall be your rear guard."* The healing that will break forth is the removal of your coping mechanisms which is only possible through a miracle of creation power known as your Genesis Moment. It is the moment when God destroys all your imperfect lovers and sets Himself up as your first love.

Once your healing springs up speedily, the verse says *your righteousness shall go before you*, in the diagram this is pictured by the arrow proceeding from God in the form of His power. Though Isaiah 64:6 says that our own attempts at righteousness are as filthy rags; the righteousness of God now goes out to the world through you and is seen as the fruit of the Spirit in your

141

interaction with others. In the first diagram, the world only sees the symptoms of a much larger problem in your heart and categorizes them as sin or religion. When the heart is set free and the fruit of the Spirit is experienced by others through their encounters with you, they no longer see the symptoms of sin or religion, but rather they see the transformational work of the Holy Spirit.

The fruit of the Spirit that people encounter through you produces praise and honor. One of the principles taught in the Bible is that we are to honor others above ourselves (Romans 12:10). Along with that principle must come the understanding that the person being honored must also know how to receive that honor with thanksgiving and humility.

Too many people today shun honor in a show of false humility because they have never been able to receive honor. When the people in our lives view the work of God, they often praise the work He does. When God worked through the lives of Paul and Barnabas in Lystra by healing someone through their ministry, the people went overboard calling them gods. The people tried to worship Paul and Barnabas, which is never acceptable to God. Paul and Barnabas tore their clothes and pleaded with the people not to worship them but to worship God. In this case the people were deceived and worshiped the vessel instead of God.

No one should ever seek the honor or glory that only God is worthy to receive. However, when God works through our lives and someone praises His work through us, a simple "thank you" is all the response that is necessary. At the same time you receive the praise, your heart should be acknowledging that God's grace is the power in your life that people are witnessing. God has now caught you in His cycle of love. Your heart is being filled with

142

significance and security from people who are experiencing God's power through your life as He displays the fruit of His Spirit.

This exchange is only possible through the Holy Spirit. By simply responding to honor with a "Thank you", you are now receiving God's love because He is making your life significant and secure. God is allowing His power to fill your heart with value, which is love, while you ultimately know that only Jesus is the source. He will always be your only source of self-worth and contentment. This is His fulfillment of the last half of Isaiah 58:8 because His glory is now your rear guard.

As your grow forward from this point, you will care less and less about the filling of your own heart, and you will care more and more about His righteousness going forth from you. Jesus had no thought of Himself. He did all that He did for His Father. His Spirit is alive in us today as the Holy Spirit and so we should not expect that He would do anything differently as He lives through us. He is completely transforming your heart into His and your reward is true love.

The point of the free heart is to enter into the true love of God and to realize it is only His righteousness through you that fills your heart with significance and security. This cycle of receiving love and value through God's work causes you to seek Him first as your hunger for Him and His presence grows!

If you follow the arrow in the diagram from your heart to God you will see that it is the only response for which you are responsible. The rest of the arrows and outcomes represent Jesus's responsibility to His Word and work. Before experiencing your own Genesis Moment you would have grabbed onto your coping mechanisms first because the lies created a hindrance to returning to Him. Now He is your first response. The value that He gives your heart through the whole process continues to create a greater desire for Jesus alone – because now you know that without Him as the source you will be empty.

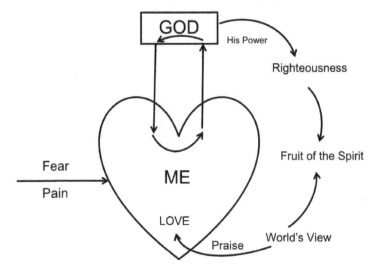

Romans 6:17-18 "We have become slaves to righteousness...

No Coping Mechanisms

The diagram pictures the beautiful circle of the righteous bondservant, and that is what Isaiah 58:8 says, "...*the glory of the Lord shall be your rear guard,*" God's glory is what keeps you in the circle of His righteousness. Romans 6:17-18 says, *"But thanks be to God, that you who were once slaves of sin have become obedient from the heart to the standard of teaching to which you were committed, and, having been set free from sin, have become slaves of righteousness."* This is exactly what the freedom diagram is declaring and what the freedom of your heart will bring.

Your former coping mechanisms were your slavery to sin that you couldn't shake even if you wanted to. It was not possible under your own efforts to change and so you were unable to be obedient from the heart. Your heart was trapped in bondage to sin. But once the freedom of your heart is granted by God, you are now made a slave of righteousness. You are held in the circle of the diagram because you continue to be guarded by the glory of the Lord. Your Genesis Moment results in an addiction to the holiness of Jesus Christ.

As the Lord grants you the freedom of your heart it is critical that you do not let your guard down or give way to pride by thinking that you have arrived. As I stated before, being set free is not arrival, but it is the point from which the rest of your Christian walk can grow. We are like the lame man; unless Jesus heals us we cannot walk with Him in the relationship He desires. So the commandments of God's Word must continue to be followed in your life. You must continue to walk in compassionate obedience with the Lord every day. You must continue to confess if and when you fall into sin. It is through your obedience that your relationship will continue to grow deeper and deeper with the Lord. Let Him take you deeper.

A Growing Love

How can you seek after a perfect God who loves you so much that He destroys the chains that bind and sets your heart free to walk intimately with Him? Only by working on your side of the relationship, Philippians 2:12 says *"Therefore, my beloved, as you have always obeyed, so now, not only as in my presence but much more in my absence, work out your own salvation with fear and trembling,"*. Once free, the desire for sin leaves because it is replaced by a desire for the One we love. To hate anything we must first love something. When we love God, we hate sin. God is holy, we must be holy. As we love God, we love holiness and it

145

is the Spirit of holiness that replaces our coping mechanisms. Because we hate sin we chase after the righteous things of God because we know He alone is our fulfillment.

To seek the perfect God in love we must follow 2 Corinthians 7:1 *"Since we have these promises, dear friends, let us purify ourselves from everything that contaminates body and spirit, perfecting holiness out of reverence for God."* This means it is time for you to throw away the things that will contaminate your body or spirit. There is no way to become too holy, but there is always a way to be too worldly.

Hebrews 12:1-2 says this, *"Therefore, since we are surrounded by such a great cloud of witnesses, let us throw off everything that hinders and the sin that so easily entangles, and let us run with perseverance the race marked out for us. [2]Let us fix our eyes on Jesus, the author and perfecter of our faith, who for the joy set before him endured the cross, scorning its shame, and sat down at the right hand of the throne of God."* You must be surrounded by such a great cloud of witnesses. You must stay active in the body of Christ. You must let Jesus be the author of your faith, meaning you let Him write the story and you just live it.

To seek God in love you must strive to be blameless in your communication with Him. 1 Thessalonians 5:17 says, *"Pray without ceasing."* We must never stop communicating with God – He wants an ongoing conversation with each of His children. That means speaking and listening. He tells us over and over to arise in the morning to hear His voice. He wants us to communicate with him.

In Hebrews 5:14 says, *"But solid food is for the mature, who by constant use have trained themselves to distinguish good from evil."* God desires that you will use His word constantly. He commands you to hide it in your heart that you might not sin against Him. As you enter this intimate relationship with the Lord, the Bible is no longer a book of rules you "ought" to read. It becomes a love letter you cannot wait to read, that you desire to read, that you crave – every word and phrase takes on a new meaning for the One you love. If you truly love God, you will keep the Bible constantly before you. What He puts into you through your reading and meditation comes back out of your heart because it is engraved in your innermost being.

We must secondly strive to be blameless in our service to God. Romans 12:11 says this, *"Never be lacking in zeal, but keep your spiritual fervor, serving the Lord."* God wants you to always have the unquenchable fire in your chest to serve Jesus. It does not mean doing things we think Jesus wants us to do, but rather serving Him as Mary did with the fine perfume; pouring ourselves out every day to bless His heart. The only way you will maintain that fire for the Lord is to always be serving the Lord. In everything you do, you need to do it in word or deed, as unto Jesus Christ as the Holy Spirit reveals in Colossians 3:17.

You must follow the example of Jesus Christ of which was said in John 21:21, *"Jesus did many other things as well. If every one of them were written down, I suppose that even the whole world would not have room for the books that would be written."* Every day you will have opportunities to show the world the compassion and love of Jesus – you must take every opportunity.

Finally, you must strive to be blameless in your intimacy with God. You must pray for opportunities in which you can help others through compassion that only God will see. These are your intimate moments with your Creator.

Matthew 6:1-4 is clear about the way to be intimate with God, *"Be careful not to do your 'acts of righteousness' before men, to be seen by them. If you do, you will have no reward from your Father in heaven. So when you give to the needy, do not announce it with trumpets, as the hypocrites do in the synagogues and on the streets, to be honored by men. I tell you the truth, they have received their reward in full. ³But when you give to the needy, do not let your left hand know what your right hand is doing, ⁴so that your giving may be in secret. Then your Father, who sees what is done in secret, will reward you."* God also desires to be ever present with you intimately as Proverbs 3:6 says, *"in all your ways acknowledge him, and he will make your paths straight."* He desires you intimately. Allow your mind to take you to that transcendent place where Jesus Christ is more fulfilling that even your strongest earthly desires. Let Him be your *"I AM!"*

My friend Tom had chosen baseball as his first love; in baseball he will never find true contentment. Rather, contentment will only be found in confession, compassion, and repentance as he returns to Jesus. This is also the only way Tom will ever be filled with the significance and security he was designed for. It is the only way he, or any of us, will be able to find our identity, self-worth, and value.

As the perfect Lover, God does not require you to win every time in order to be loved, nor does He put conditions on you for the love He wants you to receive. It is not because of your actions that you can become the lover that God desires you to be. It is only by God's power that your heart can become a heart of flesh able to enter the intimate relationship of love with Him, which is the way He intended it from the beginning. It is His power, but it is also your responsibility. You must choose to obey Him because you love him. You must choose to be compassionate because you love Him. You must choose to admit to and commit to the pain you experience because you love and trust Him to make all things new. 2 Corinthians 5:17 says, *"Therefore, if anyone is in Christ, he is a new creation; the old has gone, the new has come!"* It's time to rejoice in your own Genesis Moment for the heart set free!

Assignment

As you conclude this chapter I trust the Lord is filling you more and more with the understanding of His matchless love and unending grace. He is relentless in His pursuit of those who will worship Him in Spirit and in Truth. As you continue to replace the lies in your life with the Truth there is another practical assignment that can help you in the journey. As you learned in this chapter, in order to hate something, you must first love something more. As you are experiencing this new heart of flesh and you are finding ways to keep it from damage, you must still allow the lies to be rooted out. There will still be some pain during recovery, but now instead of running and hiding from the pain with your coping mechanisms you will allow the pain to bring change which will draw you closer to your first love.

The assignment is for you to go to your team, your accountability partner, your spouse, and anyone else that may have joined in this journey with you. Have each member of your team write you a letter that truthfully points out what would happen in the future if your coping mechanisms were not eliminated. Many people think their coping mechanisms are not a big deal because they don't affect anyone else. Unfortunately, the reality is that coping mechanisms are detrimental to the people in your life, just as much as they are in your own life. Encourage your team to be blunt and honest – you want people who will not pull any punches, but will speak the truth as honestly as they can. Once they have written the letter, you must have them read it to you so you can hear from their own mouth how destructive your coping mechanisms were.

For me this assignment was very difficult. I read about this in David Clarke's book *Six Steps to Emotional Freedom* and I followed through with it.[xiii] At the time I went to my mentor and leader in the church and asked him to write a letter that explained clearly what would happen in my life if my coping mechanisms continued to control me. The second part of this assignment is equally as tough. There is something that occurs when you hear someone's voice as they speak truth into your life.

This assignment will help you to hate the sin even more, and that is the point. As my mentor read his letter to me and spoke of how I would cease to ever be effective for the kingdom, how I would never experience a Godly marriage or relationship, and how people would never be able to trust me, etc. my heart broke and I began to see the sin the way God wanted me to see it. He wants us to hate it because it keeps us from knowing His love.

I believe you will find in your life that God is more than capable of being your first love and keeping you in the cycle of righteousness and creating in you a holy addiction. I am excited for you as you continue to walk through the hard work of following Christ. The reward is so great, not just the rewards in heaven, but the rewards of the here and now.

In the next chapter we will look into the Word and see what God has to say about the heart's greatest enemy – Satan. Winning wars is only possible for those who understand their enemy. God has spoken much about our enemy so that we don't have to lose the battles or the war any longer.

Reflections:

1. Did you google Laminin? If you never have, take just a few minutes to look into the intimate way God has created every human being.

2. Do you still have fears that you could list? If so list 3 in order of intensity. Now compare them with the list of fears you had listed from your reflections following chapter 4.

3. Take a moment to write down three of the promises from God's Word that you found most encouraging in this last chapter and meditate upon what He is saying to you through His Word.

Chapter 8

A Powerless Enemy Winning

Wars are won or lost based upon the understanding of the enemy. When a military force understands how the enemy moves, defeating that enemy becomes a matter of time. In the realm of spiritual matters this is also true. Our enemy, the devil, is seeking whom he may devour and many times we are not paying any attention. We have touched on this a number of times throughout this book, but here we will unpack some more of God's Word that will continue to help establish the firm foundation your heart needs. The enemy is relentless in pursuing God's creation. Unfortunately today too many followers of Christ fail to understand their enemy and fail to have victory in their lives.

The victory over sin and death and the devil came through the cross of Jesus Christ. A transfer was made at the moment that Jesus declared *"It is finished!"* Colossians 2:13-15 says, *"And you, who were dead in your trespasses and the uncircumcision of your flesh, God made alive together with him, having forgiven us all our trespasses, by canceling the record of debt that stood against us with its legal demands. This he set aside, nailing it to the cross. He disarmed the rulers and authorities and put them to open shame, by triumphing over them in him."* The verbs in this first passage are spoken in the past tense identifying the victory of the cross. Our faith in Jesus Christ also aligns us with this victory and creates a transfer in our life from the old flesh into the new circumcision of the heart. Without a transfer from the old into the new, there is no deliverance. This point has to be made because of the severity of missing the freedom offered in Christ – there are many to whom Jesus will say, *"I never knew you, get away from me you workers of iniquity."*

According to John 8: 34-38, *"Jesus replied, 'I tell you the truth, everyone who sins is a slave to sin. Now a slave has no permanent place in the family, but a son belongs to it forever. <u>So if the Son sets you free, you will be free indeed.</u>"* (underline added by author) Sinning is unacceptable before an almighty God and is not what Christ intended for any believer when he died for sin on the cross. Unfortunately the enemy of the cross has been at work, and he is doing a masterful job of trapping innocent hearts through coping mechanisms.

The rulers of darkness may lose their grip on the eternal souls of people who get saved, but that does not prevent the enemy from the onslaught of attacks. Just to render a believer ineffective will help the enemy's cause of preventing others from being saved. Once the heart is trapped sufficiently in a coping mechanism, the work of temptation that the enemy has to engage in is drastically reduced. No longer does temptation need to be constant because any perceived pain or fear of pain will be quickly soothed by coping mechanisms. In this way the enemy knows that such a person is rendered ineffective for the kingdom of God and is what Romans 6:17 declares *"...a slave to sin."* Our enemy is far superior to humans in cunning and knowledge and thus uses the generations of hurt people to continue to trap the hearts of their children in coping mechanisms.

This is why we must always connect our compassionate obedience with evangelism. To evangelize means to proclaim the good news. The victory and freedom that are offered through a relationship with Jesus Christ is good news to every soul who will believe. It is our responsibility to proclaim that truth to each person as the Lord grants us the opportunity. We are God's ambassadors to this world. We are to be His disciples going into the entire world preaching the gospel and baptizing people in the name of the Father, Son, and Holy Spirit and teaching them to obey all that Jesus commanded, and Jesus said, *"I will be with you to the very end of the age."* We have nothing to fear.

As you are beginning to experience this new freedom, Jesus declares His victory over the enemy in your heart. He will continue to build up His love in you so that evangelism will become a natural outflow. Telling others about Jesus when you don't have the love that freedom brings is extremely difficult. But sharing the good news of love, freedom, and contentment offered in Jesus once your life is living proof, is as natural as breathing. As you continue this journey, do not just live compassionately, but also share the Gospel when the Lord affords you the opportunity – after all, our enemy is defeated and has been for 2000 years.

Satan's Start

Genesis 3:15 says, *"And I will put enmity between you and the woman, and between your offspring and hers; he will crush your head, and you will strike his heel."* God is speaking to Satan in the garden after his deception of Adam and Eve. Satan in the form of a serpent played a role in bringing sin into the world. The Word tells us that there will be a struggle between mankind and Satan. This struggle will continue between his offspring and the children of men until the very end of the ages. However, God claims the victory for Himself here in this verse. Though Satan will be allowed to strike the heel of man (a non-mortal wound), the seed of woman will ultimately crush his head (Jesus delivering

154

a deadly blow). The infliction of pain here is obviously not fatal for man, but results in damnation for Satan. Anyone knows that bruising a heel will not kill a man. In contrast, everyone also knows that crushing the head is fatal.

Why must we work to set our hearts and the hearts of others free from bondage? Because right now Satan appears to be winning this battle. We know in the end that God will be victorious over him, but Hosea 4:6 says, *"My people are destroyed for lack of knowledge; because you have rejected knowledge, I reject you from being a priest to me. And since you have forgotten the law of your God, I also will forget your children."* I believe that unless we proclaim the truth of God's Word in helping others be set free God will repeat the judgments once brought upon the wicked and rebellious nations, and He will do it right here in America. God's heart is merciful and mercy must be our heartbeat as well. Though the book of Revelation declares God's final judgments, until that day He is still patient as no one understands patience and desires that everyone should come to repentance and that none should perish (2 Peter 3:9).

How has Satan been so successful in stealing people's hearts? As we have discussed in the previous chapters, he has trapped hearts by convincing them of lies. He has worked to hurt people and convince them that even God's love is something they needs to deal with through coping mechanisms. He has blinded man to the real problem – the heart condition. Once men's hearts were trapped by the flaming arrows of the evil one, they could do nothing else but trap the hearts of their children.

In Ephesians 6, Paul tells us of the importance of the armor of God, *"For our struggle is not against flesh and blood but against the rulers, against the authorities, against the spiritual forces of evil in the heavenly realms. Therefore put on the full*

155

armor of God, so that when the day of evil comes, you may be able to stand your ground, and after you have done everything, to stand. Stand firm then with the belt of truth buckled around your waist, with your breastplate of righteousness in place and with your feet fitted with the readiness that comes from the gospel of peace. In addition to all this, take up the shield of faith, with which you can extinguish all the flaming arrows of the evil one. Take the helmet of salvation and the sword of the Spirit, which is the word of God." The armor God provides is directly related to the attack of our enemy.

Vision of Armor

One day the Lord provided a vision of what this armor looks like in a person's life. This is a portion of Scripture that I pray every day when I wake up. I have learned the hard way that without this armor, I am often open to the attacks of the enemy who will attempt to sway me from the course of living in abundant love with Jesus. The vision began in ancient Roman where a man was rising from his bunk wearing nothing more than his undergarments. He went from his bunk into a long tunnel – it was the tunnel leading to the gladiators' arena. Along the way he came to a place where the armor hung on the wall. The armor was provided, but it was his responsibility to put it on. Once he put on the armor he continued to a table of weapons – there he picked up the shield of faith, the helmet of salvation and the sword of the Spirit. He had selected his weapons of choice and was almost ready to enter the arena.

But before he could enter there were others before him and so he was allowed to sit on a narrow bench along the wall just in front of the gates to the arena. It was there that someone coached him in the battle that was about to ensue. Then it was his turn and he began to walk to those gates – he could see the light shimmering across the dust through the gapped boards. What awaited him on the outside was still a mystery, yet he knew that he was prepared as he donned his armor and meditated on the instruction. Then just before the gates opened, Jesus Christ stepped in front of him and commanded with a roaring voice, *"Open the Gate."* Jesus looked back at the man who was now dressed and prepared and said *"Follow me."* The vision revealed that the fight belongs to Jesus and He guarantees the victory. Exodus 14:14 says, *"The Lord will fight for you, and you have only to be silent."*

The armor of God's Word is there hanging up every morning, waiting for you to put it on. He has given us weapons to wield. But He has also given us instruction through his Word that we must understand before we try and fight. Many will skip the time of soaking in God's Word and wonder why the battles are so defeating. Unless a man is soaked in God's Word and instruction, his temporary defeats are inevitable. Too many believers today fail to see the importance of putting on the armor and they walk down that hallway in nothing more than their undergarments and enter the arena totally unprepared. Is it any wonder the enemy is having success? We are told in Romans 12 to renew our minds daily. There is no shortcut to this love relationship with Jesus Christ – we must read and meditate on His Word daily.

The Armor of the Heart

The first piece of armor is the belt of truth buckled around our waist. How does this relate to the diagram of the free heart?

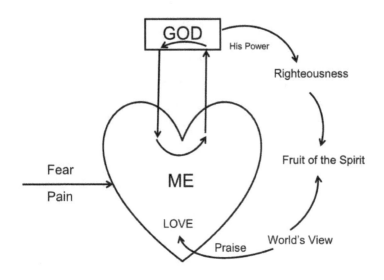

Romans 6:17-18 "We have become slaves to righteousness...

No Coping Mechanisms

Freedom from your coping mechanisms came when you replaced Satan's lies with the Truth. The belt of truth is the cycle of the holy addiction created through freedom that is represented by the circle that proceeds from God in the diagram. Your heart was created by God, is valuable to God, and is designed to be in a love relationship of intimacy with Jesus Christ. Nothing the enemy can tell you now can defeat the position you have in Jesus Christ. You are fully encompassed with the truth that God's love is sufficient for all the significance and security you will ever need. That truth buckled around you will protect you from the lies of the enemy and is represented by the arrow from your heart back to God no matter what comes your way.

The second piece of armor is the breastplate of righteousness. This piece of armor is found in the relationship we have with Christ. Galatians 2:20 says, *"I have been crucified with*

Christ. It is no longer I who live, but Christ who lives in me. And the life I now live in the flesh I live by faith in the Son of God, who loved me and gave himself for me." The breastplate is Jesus' life covering your life. He is your protection – He is the one walking out into the arena of life in front of you. His presence in your life is maintained by continual confession and obedience. Put on this armor by confessing your sins and laying bare the breastplate of His righteousness. Too many people today are putting on garments of sin over their breastplate and hiding it from sight. We are to be known by His presence and the shine of His breastplate will let the enemy know who we belong to.

The third piece of armor is the gospel of peace fitted on our feet. Romans 10:15 says the feet of those who go and preach the gospel are beautiful. Our armor again is not intended for selfish protection alone, but is to prepare us for helping others to know their own victory over the enemy. Peace with God means war with the enemy, but God will ensure that you will become an ambassador of Christ in sharing the truth about salvation and freedom in Jesus Christ. Your life will be an example of the fruit of the Spirit as we see in the diagram of the free heart.

The fourth portion of armor is the first weapon. It is a weapon of defense, the shield of faith. This shield can also be recognized in the diagram of the free heart as the entire circle from your heart to God, His power going forth, your life bearing fruit and helping others, others hearing of his love, people praising His work through your life while your heart is being filled with greater love, which is why you return right back to Him. The process will go on and on. This can only begin by faith. Without faith it is impossible to please God. No matter what the enemy tries to throw at this cycle it will only bring greater love for God as you use each opportunity of difficulty to trust in your first love, Jesus

Christ. This is why James said, *"Resist the devil and he will flee from you."* When you are turning the devil's attempts to defeat you into God's praise he will cease to fuel that fire and thus the shield of faith will extinguish and deflect the flaming arrows of the evil one.

Prior to freedom and without this armor, when the arrows hit their mark in the hearts of our forefathers, there was no longer a way for them to take up the shield of faith. The word faith does not exist in the Hebrew as "faith," the word in the Hebrew is actually "faithfulness." Faith is not a noun. Faith is not something you can possess by itself. Faith is a verb and is only found in faithfulness. To say you are a person of faith without faithfulness is a lie. James is clear in chapter 2 verse 26, *"As the body without the spirit is dead, so faith without deeds is dead."*

This is the "wholeheartedness" we read of in Romans 6. Living a life that desires to be blameless will allow God to show you and grow you in every place you oppose Him. And as God through Paul clearly states in Ephesians 6, the shield of faith must be taken up to extinguish the flaming arrows of the evil one. A heart that is trapped in a sin pattern can neither put on the shield of faith in their own life, nor put on the shield of faith in the lives of their children. Satan attacked the source and found a way to strike the heel of man so that every generation born after a generation of trapped hearts will be a replication of the generation before. He no longer has to attack and tempt because he has already successfully laid hold of the one thing that God desires more than anything – man's heart.

The fifth piece of armor is also a weapon of protection – the helmet of salvation. This helmet protects the mind. The Word says that it was our heel that would be bruised, but it was Satan's head that would be crushed. Satan continues to try and tell lies to

God's children so that if they will simply believe for a moment, they will lose their bearing on truth. When a child of God loses bearing on the Truth, the way becomes lost and difficult, filled with despair. The armor must be put on so that we can have the mind of Christ placed within us by the power of the Spirit. It is the Spirit of God who will grant us the mind of Christ, who is never deceived by the enemy's lies. This helmet will keep our minds pure and protected.

The last piece of the armor is the sword of the Spirit which is the word of God. The word of God referenced here is the *rhema* of God. This is a Greek word meaning that is not just a written word, but that is a personal and applied word or a word lived in the life of the person receiving it. The *rhema* of God is a word He has made personal in your life. It is the word written on your heart. It may be a prophetic word from another person regarding God's call on your life. Such a word must always be in line with the principles and commands of God's written Word. These *rhema* words need to be taken up to remembrance as they form God's purpose and plan for your life. The Logos of God for all people is that Jesus will set the captive free – for some it will become *rhema* which is what I believe God is doing in your life. When freedom is granted to your heart, the *rhema* of John 8:36 rings true and will become your weapon when you speak it, *"So if the Son sets you free, you will be free indeed."*

Fight for the Children

Think back on Johnny's story to remember how easily his heart was trapped and crushed to the point that he knew nothing else but to fight to protect what little bit he had left? The harder he tried to protect the more trapped he became. I was also that little boy who was left to protect my own heart but tried to do it without God's truth. More and more throughout the generations, the hearts of our forefathers were trapped. You see, it wasn't always the enemy's activity tempting people to sin – it was also the wickedness and the trap of their own hearts that created their own coping mechanisms to protect their hearts, and that carried future generations into strongholds of sin.

Well, now is the time to tell the truth. Now is the time to set the hearts of men and women all over this world free so that they will no longer live as slaves of sin, but that they will take back the generations for the Lord. Jesus made us for a great purpose and He wants us to fulfill that purpose through Him. He doesn't just want us to be saved to escape the flames, but rather He wants us to live life abundantly and free from the burden of sin.

I want you to close your eyes and I want you to picture a young child that you know very well. I want you to see their sweet smile and their innocent laugh. I want you to see their carefree joy and childlike faith as they play. See the twinkle in their eye that melts your heart.

Now picture the enemy with a smile on his face. See his perverse smirk and the arrogance in his stare. Watch him put his arm around that little child. As the trusting child looks at the enemy no one has told the child who he is or what his intention is. The child doesn't know any better and turns to go with him. As the enemy turns, he looks back over his shoulder at you and licks his lips in victory as he sweeps that child away.

You know that he is going to abuse that child, rape that child, and throw the child away into a cold dark prison - alone. He will put all the blame on the shoulders of that child for every pain the child feels. He will stop at nothing to convince the child that the only way to live is to fight for protection and strive to find relief through the world's system. The child is left alone and screaming for someone to help, but no one is helping.

People just keep walking by; they don't care about the children because they are blinded by their own pain. After all, they were once that child. So child after child continues to be destroyed, raped, abused, crushed, captured and trapped, and no one is doing anything about it. We go about our religious lives not even paying attention to what is truly happening around us. God's heart continues to be broken as his creation continues moving further away.

Deceit

The most important truth you must understand about Satan and his desire to destroy is that he does not want any heart to be set free. A generation of people addicted to Jesus' holiness would be devastating to his schemes. When a heart gets close to being set free, he will go back to his language of lies. He wants people to believe that there is no need for freedom. He will convince them that there is no need to uncover the past. But he will also work to convince them that their sin is too much for Jesus' love. He is a liar and the father of lies. He comes as an angel of light, 2 Corinthians 11:14 says, *"And no wonder, for Satan himself masquerades as an angel of light. It is not surprising then, if his servants masquerade as servants of righteousness. Their end will be what their actions deserve."*

Too many times the people who come for counseling believe a devastating lie. They are convinced that there is no need to really go through the whole process of setting their hearts free. One of Satan's famous lies is that the heart is fine just where it is.

He will convince the person that they have had a tremendous spiritual break through, and no longer have a need to see their heart set free. People have often told me during counseling that they "get it" now and "understand what was wrong". Yet it is not a matter of understanding, it is a matter of receiving a miracle from God through the power of the Holy Spirit. Humility is missing when someone believes this lie and still remains trapped. One such case is worth sharing.

One of the men I had met with came to me during one of our sessions and couldn't wait to share something he had read in God's Word that week. He explained how he had gotten alone with God one night and was reading the story of Samuel in 1 Samuel 3 when God calls to Samuel and Samuel does not understand God's voice. Eli finally recognizes what is happening and tells Samuel how to respond to God's audible call. The young man looked at me with wonder and excitement and said something like, "I am Samuel. I know I said I wanted to find freedom for my heart, but really I figured it out; I just wasn't hearing God when he was calling. I was listening to myself and letting sin creep in."

The Lord used this to teach me a profound lesson. Instead of discouraging him with advice, I chose to encourage him in his revelation that sometimes we really do not listen to God because we are too busy listening to ourselves. However, the night before he and I met, the Holy Spirit had prompted me to read my journal entry dated 6 months before the day of my own Genesis Moment. In that entry I wrote almost the exact words that I heard from this young man that morning. In my journal I praised God for setting me free during a time of prayer the night before and I professed in that same entry that He was everything to me at that moment. I turned a few pages in that journal and read another journal entry just a few days later where I had fallen back into my coping mechanism and was yet again begging God for mercy and forgiveness and professing my desire to change. I paged ahead and saw the same pattern emerge six different times from the pages of my own journal over the course of those six months.

I quickly realized by reading those entries that it was deception that was holding me captive and keeping me from a heart transformation. Satan was happy that I would go to a church service and cry and pray at the altar and thank God for freedom because he knew that my head would tell my heart a lie. Since my heart was still trapped in coping mechanisms, it was still deceitfully wicked above all else as Jeremiah 17:9 declares. A trapped heart will continue to tell the mind that everything is OK, and in the process, continue to reach for the coping mechanism every time it feels threatened. This is the arrogance of the heart that must be purged out through confession.

This young man was also being deceived in the same way. He was experiencing a mind enlightenment, that went no deeper, and left his heart to fend for itself. That morning I shared with him how God had prompted me to read those journal entries just the night before we met. The Holy Spirit is always at work, because for some reason I had also brought that journal with me that morning and was able to read those entries to him. Unfortunately, he saw how that applied to me, but he did not believe it applied to him and continued to battle his coping mechanisms on his own.

As an angel of light, Satan wants men and women to believe in apparent victories because it will ultimately keep them from experiencing real victory. It is critical that you understand this so that you can fend off his attacks and his deceit and press on toward greater freedom. For others, it may not be just mental enlightenment that the enemy uses, it may be as Mark 4:15 says,

"Some people are like seed along the path, where the word is sown. As soon as they hear it, Satan comes and takes away the word that was sown in them." You must be on guard and aware that the enemy is going to be very active as people begin to enter into true love with Jesus Christ.

The enemy will no longer have a "fool-proof" way of trapping the children's hearts and his destruction will be put to an end. He hates nothing more than to be defeated. God warns us to be on guard in 1 Peter 5:8-9, *"Be self-controlled and alert. Your enemy the devil prowls around like a roaring lion looking for someone to devour. Resist him standing firm in the faith, because you know that your brothers throughout the world are undergoing the same kind of sufferings."*

Just as you have walked toward your own Genesis Moment and into a holy addiction, it is time for you to be praying that God will lead you to some people who are also prepared to begin this adventure. You must become a disciple maker and one of the best ways you can fulfill that calling is to walk through this same process with someone else. The reason God comforts you with a heart set free is that you might bring hope to someone living with a trapped heart in need of rescue. Don't forget, we are His ambassadors! Not only will you have the reward of seeing someone else set ablaze for Jesus Christ, but you will earn an eternal reward for your obedience in making disciples. Walk with others to help them dispel lies in their lives and it will help you in return to do the same.

Legal Right

One of the tactics of the enemy is to approach the souls of men through their sin. When a person engages in sins of the soul there is a place of legal right that the enemy claims in that person's life. Sins of sexual immorality, sins of divination, sins of sorcery, and sins of drug and alcohol abuse can create a legal right for the enemy to approach your soul through the avenues you opened. There are many believers today that have sinned profusely in these ways before coming to Christ. One of the ways to continue resisting the devil, is to cut off these paths of legal right the enemy once had in your life. Neil Anderson wrote a book called *Bondage Breaker*[xiv] that directly addresses these struggles and strongholds. I would highly recommend that you read and apply the teachings he brings forth in the book. But here and now you can also take away the enemy's legal right over your life.

In Matthew 12:43-45, Jesus proclaimed the danger of the return of the unclean spirits to the house they once occupied. If the house is swept clean and put in order but is empty, the unclean spirits will return sevenfold to occupy the house. It is your responsibility to cut off this legal right by filling up your spiritual house with the Truth and occupancy of Jesus Christ and not just by sweeping it clean. Many of those who have pursued their Genesis Moment have experienced difficulty in removing the memory of sexual sin from their minds. As long as the legal right remains, the enemy will be able to access your life in these areas and bring turmoil. However, Jesus Christ desires that all of those avenues be cut off and all the ammunition of the enemy be removed from our lives.

The first thing you can do is to pray through 1 John 5:18 and renounce all the ways in your life that the enemy has touched you. While you pray through this verse and ask God to reveal and remove any oppression the enemy has brought into your life there may be many distractions and difficulties that suddenly come up. As you pray and find yourself getting tongue tied and feeling like your brain is going blank, open your Bible to the book of Ephesians and just begin to read out loud. The Lord uses His Word to revive the soul (Psalm 19:7) and it will bring you back to a place that you can begin praying once again. Continue to renounce any of the enemy's activity that the Holy Spirit reveals and repent of it, but also replace it with the truths from God's Word that you have read and learned along this journey. You will find this to be one of the most freeing things you can do.

God wants you free of the enemy's grip in every area of your life and He will provide you the protection during this process. Remember we do not have an enemy that is powerful since he was rendered powerless by the Cross. He was defeated at the cross and he only has power over people who give him authority. Do not agree with the enemy, but agree with God, confess your sin and declare His truth, and true love will flow in and through your heart like springs of living water.

One final process that I went through with the Lord personally was sitting down during a time of fasting and prayer and asking God to bring back to my memory every act of sexual immorality that I had ever committed. It was a frightening thing to ask God, but I wanted there to be nothing in my life that the enemy could use to come against me or my wife. I went through this process just a few weeks before being married and I know that God yet again granted me another level of freedom which has also provided tremendous freedom and contentment in my marriage.

I knew that my sexual encounters had allowed the enemy an avenue into my life that needed to be cut off. In many cases I wasn't sure if I would remember each instance. Amazingly over a period of about 3 days the Lord brought to memory each situation. Some had been long forgotten, but that didn't mean that the enemy couldn't still have access through them at some time in the future. My desire was to cut off all possible routes for the enemy.

Once I had compiled a list of names or situations I sat down and confessed each situation to a brother and asked God to renounce any spirit that once had access to my life through those situations. I called each situation out just as God said it was – if it was sexual intercourse then I declared that aloud and repented, if it was immorality then I declared that and repented, if drunkenness or divination then the same. In each case I asked Jesus to cast those spirits and the situation into outer darkness and judgment. I can write this with total peace knowing that there is nothing in my life that I am aware of today that I have not brought out into the light of Christ to let His love wash it away forever.

This is also something you can walk through with your team or with someone who you know to be full of the Holy Spirit, someone who will pray with you for deliverance. We will talk more about the power of the Holy Spirit in the next chapter.

The truth about our enemy is that he is defeated, completely, thoroughly, and eternally. You have nothing to fear. You have a Savior that not only saved your soul from eternal death, but a Savior who saves your life today for freedom and joy abounding in an intimate relationship with Him. This freedom means the enemy has no right to you and no ammunition to throw at you. You are more than a conqueror. Put on your armor every day, sit and soak in God's Word, replace the lies with Truth and live a life of freedom in the hands of the living God by the power of the Holy Spirit through the blood of Jesus Christ.

169

Call to Action

I am praying now that you see the severity of the situation we have on our hands. Our world needs a radical change and a return to the Almighty God. The only way it can happen is if the hearts are set free to love the Lord our God with all our heart, all our soul, our entire mind, and all our strength. Only from this love relationship will it be possible to not only take up the armor in your own life, but to place the armor on your children so that you may extinguish the flaming arrows of the evil one and begin to see his head crushed beneath your feet. We all must become a people of desire, a people desiring a Holy God, desiring Holy living, desiring righteousness, and desiring heart changes in ourselves and the world around us. Then and only then will we see the end to social degradation and the rise of holiness and righteous living that God intended for each believer to experience. A generation of people addicted to the holiness of Jesus Christ.

What are the results of a heart set free? We will look at them in the next chapter and we will see that change is possible. Jesus said in Mark 9:23, *"'If you can?' said Jesus, 'Everything is possible for him who believes.'"* Only a heart set free is free to believe as Jesus' speaks.

You are reading this book now because you have a prophetic destiny in the army of God being raised up in the last days. You are called out with a purpose of divine ordering and with your heart ablaze with love for Jesus Christ, the possibilities are endless. What is God stirring within you today? No one can stop Him from seeing it through to completion. And that is what this is all about – His power, the gift of the Holy Spirit in fullness, the completion of what Christ came to do – redeem the earth and set people free.

Reflections:

1. Summarize your own feelings about the work Satan has done in your heart since you were a child. Ask Jesus to cut you off from the enemies counter attacks against the progress you have made in this journey.

2. What weapons will you use from God's Word to continue your fight against the enemies lies? List a few *rhema* words the Lord has given you.

3. Have you discovered what you are passionate about, and if so pray that the Lord will lead you to serving Him with that passion? Write down your passion and allow God to mold it into His purpose in this generation.

Chapter 9

Continual Victory

We are more than conquerors through Jesus Christ our Lord. What a beautiful blessing of God's kindness it is to be set free from the bondage that sin once had over us. There is no stronghold too strong for our Lord Jesus – His mercy will reign and break apart all bonds. Isaiah 61:1-4 declares of Jesus, *"The spirit of the Lord God is upon me; because the Lord has anointed me to bring good news to the poor; he has sent me to bind up the brokenhearted, to proclaim liberty to the captives, and the opening of the prison to those who are bound; to proclaim the year of the Lord's favor, and the day of vengeance of our God; to comfort all who mourn; to grant to those who mourn in Zion – to give them a beautiful headdress instead of ashes, the oil of gladness instead of mourning, the garment of praise instead of a faint spirit; that they may be called the oaks of righteousness, the planting of the Lord, that he may be glorified. They shall build up the ancient ruins; they shall raise up the former devastations; they shall repair the ruined cities, the devastations of many generations."* This same anointing now belongs to those whom the Son has set free.

The freedom that Christ grants is intended to continually draw us closer to Him in a life of holiness and abandon. The first commandment does not change – we must love the Lord our God with all our heart, soul, mind and strength; and our neighbor as ourselves. There is no point at which the Christian can rest upon his or her laurels and enjoy the ride. We are bondservants of our Master the Lord Jesus and that relationship must keep growing to survive. A stagnant or idle relationship is dying.

You and I have a prophetic destiny to live out in our generation. As Acts 13:36 says of David, *"For David, after he had served the purposes of God in his own generation, fell asleep and was laid with his fathers and saw corruption,"* David was a man after God's heart, Acts 13:22 says, *"And when he had removed him, he raised up David to be their king, of whom he testified and said, 'I have found in David the son of Jesse a man after my heart, who will do all my will."* You have the same call today – to be a prophetic intercessor and to fulfill God's purpose in your own generation.

Prophetic Intercession

You may be wondering what it means to be a prophetic intercessor. To be a prophetic intercessor can be defined in a number of different ways. Jim Goll in his book *"The Lifestyle of a Prophet"*[xv] gives a complete and thorough understanding of this calling. Essentially the prophetic intercessor is a saint who understands the importance of hearing and obeying the Spirit of God without reservation and without denying God's power. Amos 3:7 says, *"For the Lord God does nothing without revealing his secret to his servants the prophets."* A prophetic intercessor will take the call of listening to God's voice seriously and will allow the Spirit of God to intercede through him or her for the fulfillment of God's will. There is no special calling for this type of intercession – therefore if you are a believer today you are called. It is not by might nor by power but by the Spirit of the Lord (Zech 4:6).

173

The freedom you are experiencing with Christ is a gift that is allowing you to fulfill this call of intercession as laid out in Isaiah 61. Remember, being set free is not only for you, it is for others whom God also desires to set free. First we must proclaim the good news to the ones who do not have a relationship with Jesus Christ, and then we must proclaim the good news to those who are saved that Jesus offers freedom in Truth. The depth of the relationship that God grants to us also correlates to the degree of the responsibility we are given. We must live after His heart as King David did. Luke 12:48 says, *"But the one who did not know, and did what deserved a beating, will receive a light beating. Everyone to whom much was given, of him much will be required, and from him to whom they entrusted much, they will demand the more."* Your freedom is given to you so that you will serve God in a love relationship that creates an overflow into the world around you.

We may have known this to be true with our intellect long before we ever experienced true freedom from our coping mechanisms, but that is exactly the difference between knowledge and experience. Remember, the first temptation in the garden against Eve and Adam was to replace relationship with knowledge by eating of the tree of good and evil – to become like God – or rather to know what God knows. The heart that has not been set free from coping mechanisms can believe the lie that it is free and try to maintain the "ought to's" for Jesus in a failing attempt to love Him, but in reality it never happens because the heart is trapped in self-protection. With the coping mechanism shattered by the power of God, the heart is now free to perform its God given purpose in this generation. The freedom God declared through the prophet Isaiah promises that the glory of the Lord will be our rear guard. In Chapter 8 we looked at how this freedom

174

creates slavery to righteousness. God's power manifested through our lives results in praise from others that translates as love to our hearts all because of God's supply. The continual filling of our heart gives us a greater desire to return to Him again and again – our Genesis Moment.

The next verse, Isaiah 58:9 says, *"Then you shall call, and the Lord will answer; you shall cry, and he will say, 'Here I am.' If you take away the yoke from your midst, the pointing finger, and speaking wickedness, if you pour yourself out for the hungry and satisfy the desire of the afflicted, then shall your light rise in the darkness and your gloom be as the noonday."* The removal of the yoke from your heart is God's gift of grace based on His promise as you fulfill the commandment of His Word. Our actions are not the starting point of interaction with God – His Word is the starting point to which we respond. His Word (Promise) + our obedience = the fulfillment of His promise.

Because God promises freedom through our obedience, we obey and receive what He has declared because He cannot lie. Jesus is healing your heart and setting you free because He longs for a deeper relationship with you. Only when you experience this depth of relationship, where you taste and see that the Lord is good, will you be firmly established in a holy addiction that brings true significance and security to your heart and the contentment you've always sought. This is why we must take up the call in our generation to be prophetic intercessors – it is God's desire that all people will be saved, and that all people will be set free from the lies that bind their hearts.

175

Desires Fulfilled

The enemy of our souls has long been at work convincing the human heart of the need to fulfill its every desire. Today there are more products on the market, more drugs in the streets, more entertainment on television, more sexual encounters available, etc. than ever before in history; all of them vying for the top position in the human heart. Through this freedom found in Christ we have the evidence that only He can fulfill our greatest desires – which are the desires for significance and security. Only through Jesus will we enter into a place of transcendent relationship. He alone is the fulfillment of our desires, and though all the other offerings in this world may bring a temporary thrill, none of them can offer satisfaction to our soul.

The freedom you are experiencing from your coping mechanisms must also be guarded just like the rest of your life. The enemy of your soul will come back around at times in your life and try to gain a foothold. Oswald Chambers stated that "Unguarded strength is actually a double weakness."[xvi] Where we think we are strong we must take heed lest we fall (1 Corinthians 10:12). This does not mean that you walk in fear, but rather that you continually keep before you the truth of God's Word to dispel any lies the enemy tries to throw at you.

The promise of freedom continues in Isaiah 58:11-12, which says, *"And the Lord will guide you continually and satisfy your desire in scorched places and make your bones strong; and you shall be like a watered garden, like a spring of water, whose waters do not fail. And your ancient ruins shall be rebuilt; you shall raise up the foundations of many generations; you shall be called the repairer of the breach, the restorer of streets to dwell in."* As the Word proclaims, Jesus frees us to experience the satisfaction of our desires in the "scorched places" which gives us strength. We are called to be sustenance for those who come after us and like a watered garden, so is the heart that finds its satisfaction in Christ alone. He will use your life as a vessel to help rebuild the lives of others around you. As a slave of righteousness you no longer desire those things that oppose God, you hunger and thirst for righteousness that you might be drawn deeper into the intimacy of Christ. After all this you will want others to taste and see that the Lord is good (1 Peter 2:3) and your desire will be that they will come to know the true love offered in Jesus Christ and will experience a Genesis Moment of their own.

The promise continues in verses 13 and 14 of Isaiah 58, which says, *"If you turn back your foot from the Sabbath, from doing your pleasure on my holy day, and call the Sabbath a delight and the holy day of the Lord honorable; if you honor it, not going your own ways, or seeking your own pleasure, or talking idly; then you shall take delight in the Lord, and I will make you ride on the heights of the earth; I will feed you with the heritage of Jacob your father, for the mouth of the Lord has spoken."* The Lord is declaring His faithfulness to those who will remain faithful to Him. Rather than living to seek your own pleasure you are now free to seek the Lord's pleasure and His pleasure is Jesus. As we delight ourselves in Jesus we will be as one riding on the heights of the earth. That should be the only "High" we ever seek.

Power from Above

I've mentioned often through the writing of this book about the power available to every believer through the Holy Spirit. For many believers the Holy Spirit is known only as a title rather than the person and power of God available for life today.

Jesus wants us drawn deeper into His presence and it is only possible through the indwelling presence of His Spirit. I was a person who only knew the Holy Spirit by His title, but by His grace He continues to bring me a greater awareness of Himself. All of us need to continually be drawn closer to Jesus by the Holy Spirit. In order for some that means you will have to go through a process of unlearning.

It is difficult for human beings to unlearn things. This is why freedom from sin's bondage is so critical. All people are swayed based upon what they believe, and what people believe is the most important aspect in their life. As I stated earlier, the seed of belief produces the root of faith which sprouts into the action where the fruit is born. When beliefs stem from lies, the growth that is produced is only the fruit of death rather than the fruit of life (Romans 6:21).

To access this power that is given through the Holy Spirit we must first look at who the Holy Spirit is. The Holy Spirit is God. He is just as much God as the Father and the Son. In Chapter 1 we covered the triune nature of God. Throughout the Bible the Holy Spirit is the power and application of all that God accomplishes through men, including the power of the Holy Spirit coming upon and remaining on Jesus after His baptism in the Jordan River. You will not find Jesus performing miracles or preaching sermons in the gospels until after the Holy Spirit descends and remains upon Him. After that time, Jesus' ministry began (Luke 3:21-22).

You will also notice that Jesus is not taken into the wilderness to be tempted by the devil until He is first baptized in the Holy Spirit and then led into the wilderness for 40 days of testing (Luke 4:1-2). If it was necessary for the Son of God to need the power of God through the Holy Spirit then how much more necessary is it for you and I to need the power of God through the Holy Spirit? It is possible that still today you believe lies about the Holy Spirit. I want to ask you to be willing to let the Lord instruct you through His Word about who the Holy Spirit is, and how He will live through your life, don't just base your beliefs on what man has told you.

The Holy Spirit is first mentioned in Genesis 1:2 as hovering over the face of the waters. The Spirit of God was present at creation according to Proverbs 8. The Spirit of God came upon the men and women in the Old Testament time and time again for the purpose of accomplishing God's will. The Holy Spirit carried along all the prophets who spoke the Words of God to be recorded in the Bible according to 2 Peter 1:21. The Holy Spirit knows the deep things of God and knows the mind of God according to 1 Corinthians 2:10-11. The Holy Spirit intercedes for us when we don't know how to pray and prays the will of God on our behalf according to Romans 8:26-27. The Holy Spirit comforts the believers, convicts the believers, and reveals the things of God that would otherwise be foolishness to believers. He is the power of God in us.

The Holy Spirit now resides in the lives of every believer. The Bible records Jesus' resurrection from the dead and His appearance to the disciples at the end of the book of John. There in John 20:22, Jesus takes his disciples, except for Thomas who is absent, and breathes on them and says, *"Receive the Holy Spirit."* It is at this moment that life for the disciples begins to change and they are given the power to understand Jesus, as well as the power to carry out His purpose on earth. 1 Corinthians 6 tells us that we are the temple of the Holy Spirit. Acts 2 records the day of Pentecost following Jesus' ascension when the believers were gathered together and the Holy Spirit came and rested upon them as tongues of fire and they all began speaking in other languages as the evidence of God's power.

The Holy Spirit is the person who is responsible for giving faith to the believers according to Romans 12:3, and 1 Corinthians 2:14. The presence of faith means that God has already chosen that person to be a temple for the Holy Spirit where He immediately takes up residence.

When you read the creation account you will read in Genesis 1:11-13 that God created the vegetation and the plants according to their kind. In Genesis 1:26 you will read that God created man in His image on day 6. If you read the account of man's creation in Genesis chapter 2, you will read in verses 5-7 that man was formed from the dust of the ground before any plants or vegetation were sprouted from the ground because it had not rained and there was no man to work the ground. So if God created plants and vegetation in day 3 why were there no plants on day 6 when He was making man? The answer lies in the seed.

God made the plants and vegetation each according to its kind. God made the seeds. Remember Jesus said that unless a seed falls to the ground and dies it cannot bring forth fruit. Everything that is necessary for the life of the plant is found in the seed, and therefore all it needs is the right soil, the right sunlight, and the right water to bring forth growth. So it is with the Holy Spirit. 1 John 3:9 says, *"No one born of God makes a practice of sinning, for God's seed abides in him, and he cannot keep on sinning because he has been born of God."* The Holy Spirit is the seed of God, which contains all the power and presence of God placed within the life of each believer.

The issue is not whether the believer has the Holy Spirit, the issue is what kind of soil is the Holy Spirit planted in, what kind of water is the Holy Spirit receiving, and what exposure to the light does the Holy Spirit in a believer's life receive? The answers to those questions will reveal how much of the Holy Spirit will be manifest in a person's life. Jesus said to the woman at the well in John 4:13-14 that she only needed to drink the water He offered because it would become a spring of water welling up to eternal life. The only way she could drink is through belief.

Belief in what God says about the Holy Spirit is the water for the seed of God that dwells in you. If you don't believe what the Bible says about the Holy Spirit don't expect that seed to grow and bear much fruit.

The Bible tells us not to grieve the Holy Spirit in Ephesians 4. How will you grieve the Spirit of God? By exposing His temple to anything that is defiled. Man is not capable of exposing God the Father, Jesus, or the Holy Spirit to sin because God is perfect and sinless. However, man is able to expose God's temple to sin and defilement which is always a cause for the presence of God to depart. Matthew 6 speaks about the eye of the body being the lamp. If the lamp is dark then the whole body is made dark. This is a prime example of grieving the Holy Spirit, allowing the eye of the body to look upon sin and let it into the temple.

Galatians 5:22 gives us a list of the Fruit of the Spirit. These are not fruits as in multiple kinds, but singularly all 9 characteristics are present in the Holy Spirit simultaneously. The only way a life will be able to display this fruit is through the continual watering of the seed with belief, the continual exposure of the seed to the light (Jesus is the Light of the world), and through the supernatural growth of the Holy Spirit in the life of the believer. The question you have to answer is "Are you willing to believe all that the Bible says is possible through the power and presence of the Holy Spirit?" Are you willing to allow Him to shape your thoughts and understanding through the Word, or will you continue to rely on what you were told by others about Him?

2 Peter 1:3-4 tells us that God's divine power has given us all things that pertain to life and Godliness through the knowledge of Jesus, by which we have been granted the precious and very great promises, that we might become partakers of the divine nature which is the presence of the Holy Spirit. All God's promises are yes in Jesus according to 2 Corinthians 1:20, and Jesus said in John 16 that the Holy Spirit would come and give to each believer everything that was His. Therefore all of God's power and presence are found in the Holy Spirit that lives within you today – will you believe?

It's time that we truly give God His rightful place in the church. When God is free to be God among His people they must trust in the Lord with all their heart and lean not on their own understanding. But when God is boxed into a church's theology or creed the people cease to trust in the Lord and begin to trust in their pastor or in their own understanding.

Many churches and pastors do not really want the Holy Spirit to be in charge. We can see through Peter's submission to the Holy Spirit with Ananias and Sapphira that it is a fearful and awesome thing to let the Holy Spirit rule. But the Bible also declares that the beginning of knowledge is the fear of the Lord. Where the Spirit of the Lord is there is freedom (2 Corinthians 3:17) – and if He moves like the wind, it will be hard to lean on your own understanding. But don't be afraid, because the Lord's will is good, and pleasing, and perfect (Romans 12:2). You can trust Him to lead you.

My hope is to stir up any wrong beliefs in your life that may need to be unlearned so you can continue growing deeper into the presence of the Lord. There is no greater joy that living in freedom with Jesus Christ. If you were raised in a church who taught you things that you have never investigated through the Word of God with a humble and open heart, it is time for you to investigate.

God said the one who seeks Him with all his heart will find Him. Do not let other men's understanding hold you back from the Creator of the universe, and do not become a lone ranger who listens to no one. Rather, as the Holy Spirit instructed us all, we are to test the spirits to see that they are from God (1 John 4:1). If you will earnestly desire the greater gifts – this new found freedom you have and the power of the Holy Spirit will catapult you into Jesus' divine purpose for your life. And with a supernatural God like Jesus – there is no limit to the possibilities!

Practical Guidance

You can make the most of life's endless possibilities now through the freedom you are experiencing. The book of 2nd Peter establishes an immovable foundation for the diagram of the free heart from chapter 7. 2 Peter 1:5-8 says, *"For this very reason, make every effort to supplement your faith with virtue, and virtue with knowledge, and knowledge with self-control, and self-control with steadfastness, and steadfastness with godliness, and godliness with brotherly affection, and brotherly affection with love. For if these qualities are yours and are increasing, they keep you from being ineffective or unfruitful in the knowledge of our Lord Jesus Christ."* This passage inspired through Peter by the Holy Spirit speaks specifically about the circle of righteousness.

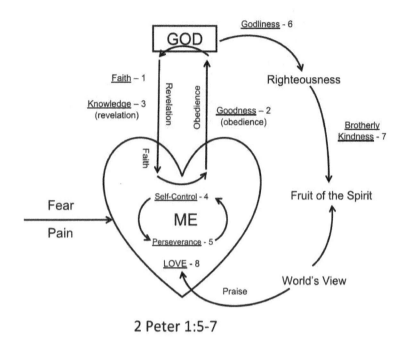

2 Peter 1:5-7

As you look at this diagram, you will notice it is much the same as the one you have already seen. The only difference here is the addition of the words from 2 Peter 1:5-8 that describe the process of living out this circle of righteousness and love in your holy addiction.

The first instruction is to add to your faith, virtue, or as the NIV translates it, *goodness*. The faith that comes from God is indicated by the arrow pointing from God into the heart of ME, so goodness or virtue is indicated by the arrow going back to God which is our obedience.

Then he says, to your virtue you are to add knowledge – Jesus told us in John 14:21 how to gain knowledge. *"Whoever has my commandments and keeps them, he it is who loves me. And he who loves me will be loved by my Father, and I will love him and*

184

manifest myself to him. " Knowledge is the manifestation of Jesus in the human heart and it is only possible through obedience which can only come through faith which is granted by the Holy Spirit. This is also evidenced by the 1st arrow which now indicates the filling of the heart with knowledge (#3) which is also called revelation.

After this, to knowledge add self-control; once you gain the knowledge of Christ, it is your responsibility to remain self-controlled by living a life of obedience to Christ in all things. To self-control you are to add steadfastness, or perseverance, as translated in the NIV. These are marked by the 4th and 5th arrows in your heart. The circle that is created is one where faith creates love, which creates obedience, obedience then grants knowledge, knowledge must be self-controlled which is obedience, and self-control must become steadfast as you persevere. The circle created by these five points has not left the intimate relationship you have with Jesus between your heart and God.

Then Peter goes on to say you must add to your steadfastness, or perseverance, godliness. What we have already learned about the heart set free is that God's righteousness goes before us as His power is manifest through our lives in our interaction with others. This godliness as witnessed by others is marked by the 6th arrow. Godliness is only experienced going out of our lives through interaction with other people and Peter says we must add to our godliness, brotherly kindness. Only when the fruit of the Spirit is truly manifested to others can brotherly kindness be of a nature that will be acceptable to God. After all, the good works of man are only as good as filthy rags (Is 64:6).

Brotherly kindness is seen in the diagram as the 7th arrow. And now when the world around you receives the fruit of the Spirit and gives you praise because of God's power, immediately your heart will be filled with significance and security that is only possible because of this transcendent relationship you now experience with your Lord and Savior Jesus Christ.

The final command is to add love to brotherly kindness. The final arrow in the diagram #8 points back to your heart because brotherly kindness toward others will result in love being added to you and fueling your holy addiction bringing you right back to your relationship with Jesus. This is the result of your Genesis Moment.

It is the love of Jesus that must compel you. It is the love of Jesus that continues to keep you free. It is the love of Jesus that pours you into the world for His glory. It is the love of Jesus that will hold you for eternity.

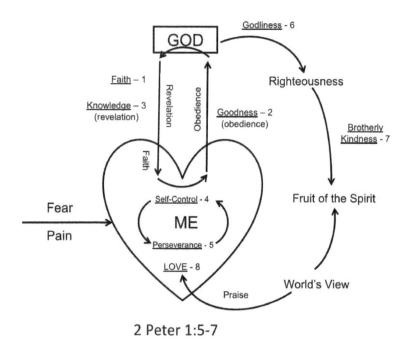

2 Peter 1:5-7

This diagram continues to show that when the right relationship with God is established in your heart, His love will always be your first priority. It is in keeping with His greatest command which is to love the Lord your God with all your heart, soul, mind, and strength – and the second is like it, which is to love your neighbor as yourself. This is also what the Holy Spirit outlined through 2 Peter 1:5-8 where we are told to work first on the relationship with our Lord and then godliness, brotherly kindness, with love being the result, much like when Jesus told you to seek first the kingdom of God and the rest will be added to you (Matthew 6:33).

Kingdom Agenda

The freedom of your heart is setting you on a course to be used at the disposal of the King of all creation. He has an agenda – an agenda to save the lost – an agenda to build up His church – an agenda to prepare His Bride for the wedding feast of the Lamb. Through the transcendent relationship you now have with your Savior your heart is content with the value Jesus has given you. Now rather than always striving to protect yourself, you can be a vessel used to supply others. You need to be the broken bread and spilled out wine that will lead them to Jesus.

Jesus said in John 7:37 *"On the last day of the feast, the great day, Jesus stood up and cried out, 'If anyone thirsts, let him come to me and drink. Whoever believes in me, as the Scripture has said, "Out of his heart will flow rivers of living water"'."* He desires that we all would have rivers of living water flowing from our hearts – hearts that have been made free by the Truth. What position have you been called to fill in the kingdom agenda? I would suggest that you not be afraid to continue seeking God in radical ways doing one part more every day. Will you take that challenge?

Jesus said that when He was gone His disciples would fast. You may want to fast for periods of time, and there are many good books that can help guide you in fasting. Fasting has been a tremendous way of building intimacy with God in my own life. The key to fasting is hearing from God. We know that Jesus taught us to fast, so when you feel led to fast – obey and step out in faith. Jesus will be faithful to speak and guide you as to the length and type of fast He desires.

One other significant way the Lord built up my intimacy and purity in Him is through the Nazarite Vow. A number of times in my walk with Christ I have felt called to follow a vow as it is described in Numbers chapter 6. Twice in Acts we see believers in the early church also setting themselves aside for God's purposes through vows like these (Acts 18:18, Acts 21:23). Whatever you hear the Lord speaking into your ears, be faithful and obey – hearing and obeying is known as the *shema* of God.

In the Old Testament the *shema* was understood by the Hebrews as "hear and obey." This is what faith meant to the Hebrew – it was an action tied to a belief – the same applies for the New Testament believer. Jesus repeated this in the New Testament many times when He made the statement *"he who has ears let him hear."* Continuing in your freedom in Christ means that you continue to listen to the One you love and do whatever He says. Today there is a lot of activity in the name of Jesus, but I believe very little of that activity has been preceded by the hearer actually hearing an assignment from the Holy Spirit. Always remember that hearing from God is the most vital part of your relationship with Him. We must tune our ears to His still small voice day after day and follow our Savior in obedience.

Jesus told us that one day He will separate the sheep from the goats. This thought takes me back to where we started – freedom begins with the humble heart – the heart that longs for God – the heart willing to live in compassionate obedience for others. Matthew 25 speaks of the final judgment and Jesus says, *"When the Son of Man comes in his glory, and all the angels with him, then he will sit on his glorious throne. Before him will be gathered all the nations, and he will separate people one from another as a shepherd separates the sheep from the goats. And he will place the sheep on his right, but the goats on the left. Then the king will say to those on his right, 'Come, you who are blessed by my Father, inherit the kingdom prepared for you from the foundation of the world. For I was hungry and you gave me food, I was thirsty and you gave me drink, I was a stranger and you welcomed me, I was naked and you clothed me, I was sick and you visited me, I was in prison and you came to me.'"*

Remember the words in Isaiah that declare the kind of fasting or obedience that God desires 1) <u>to share your food with the hungry</u>, 2) <u>to clothe the naked</u>, 3) <u>to give the poor wanderer shelter</u>, and 4) <u>not to turn your back on your own flesh and blood</u>. These are the very same things that Jesus speaks of in Matthew 25 when He says that those acts of compassionate obedience were actually done unto Him. The passage continues, *"Then the righteous will answer him, saying, 'Lord, when did we see you hungry and feed you, or thirsty and give you a drink? And when did we see you a stranger and welcome you, or naked and clothe you? And when did we see you sick or in prison and visit you?' And the King will answer them, 'Truly, I say to you, as you did it to one of the least of these my brothers, you did it to me."*

The kingdom agenda is clear and it cannot be stopped. Not even the gates of hell can prevail against it. I pray that this chapter has truly encouraged you in your walk with the Lord. There is no sweeter taste in life than the presence of Jesus Christ. He is contentment for every soul who will believe. He is the power to overcome. He is the beginning and He is the end. He is the reason you are free. I pray that you are also being given the opportunity to pass this book along to a brother, sister, friend or relative, because one of the best ways we can keep from turning our backs on our own flesh and blood is to help them find freedom in Jesus Christ. As a child of freedom in Jesus Christ you are commissioned with a mandate – Matthew 28:18-20 *"And Jesus came and said to them, 'All authority in heaven and on earth has been given to me. Go therefore and make disciples of all nations, baptizing them in the name of the Father and of the Son and of the Holy Spirit, teaching them to observe all that I have commanded you. And behold, I am with you always, to the end of the age."*

Get up, take your mat, and walk. Live life to the fullest and freest just as Jesus offers it. John 8:36 Jesus said, *"So if the Son sets you free, you will be free indeed."*

Reflections:

1. Look back at 2 Peter 1:5-7 in your Bible and identify 3 hindrances that might prevent you from following through in obedience. Ask Jesus to grant you the power to overcome those potential hindrances and remain on guard against them.

2. As you come to the conclusion of this book and begin walking in new freedom with Christ, from 1 – 10 how would you rate your level of contentment today? Look back at your answer from chapter 1 and how do they compare?

3. List some people that you would like to minister to by walking them into a Genesis Moment and the freedom of their hearts. Now start with the first person on the list and pass on the gift that God has given you.

Bibliography:

[i] Curtis, Brent; Eldredge, John, *The Sacred Romance*, (Nashville, TN; Thomas Nelson, 1997), 23.

[ii] Clarke, David E., *The 6 Steps to Emotional Freedom: Breaking Through to the Life God Wants You to Live*, (Uhrichsville, OH; Barbour Publishing, 2007), 114.

[iii] Davies, Douglas, *Child Development; A Practitioners Guide*, (New York, NY; The Guilford Press, 2004), 338.

[iv] Crabb, Dr. Larry, *Effective Biblical Counseling: A Model for Helping Caring Christians Become Capable Counselors*, (Grand Rapids, MI; Zondervan, 1977), 79-80.

[v] Simply Psychology, *Maslow's Hierarchy of Needs*, http://www.simplypsychology.org/maslow.html, (November 29, 2013).

[vi] Clarke.

[vii] Curtis; Eldredge

[viii] Ibid., 141.

[ix] Chambers, Oswald, *My Utmost for His Highest*, (Grand Rapids, MI; Discovery House, 1992), 1/31.

[x] Thompson, W. Oscar, *Concentric Circles of Concern: Seven Stages for Making Disciples*, (Nashville, TN; Broadman & Holman, 1999), 152.

[xi] Anderson, Neil T., *T-H-E Bondage Breaker: Overcoming Negative Thoughts Irrational Feelings Habitual Sins*, (Eugene, OR; Harvest House, 1993), 66.

[xii] Ibid, 36.

[xiii] Clarke, 104.

[xiv] Anderson.

[xv] Goll, James W., *The Lifestyle of a Prophet: A 21-day Journey to Embracing Your Calling*, (Minneapolis, MN; Chosen, 2013).

[xvi] Chambers.